Power of You

Publishing

CopyRight 2020

Sophia, Elijah & Quintin

Truth, Love and Patience
above all else.

Aphantasia

/def/ ***Blind In The Mind***

Discoveries - Observations - Strategies

With special reference to Mental Senses

Preface

June 27, 2020

40 years ago, ever since I was a little boy, maybe 8 or 9 years old, I
wanted to be a psychologist. Something about understanding the way
people think and act seemed like magic to me. When I began my studies
at the universities 10 years later, I quickly realized I no longer wanted
to be a "professional" psychologist. I couldn't quite find the origin of
the feeling or thoughts that made me turn against my chosen profession
but it seemed to be missing something. But when I learned towards the
end of my degree that in order to continue on, most professionals
choose a concentrated area of study, as they do in the medical
profession but also a philosophy of study. That is, a person can't
become a catholic priest by studying to be a monk anymore than a
Freudian psychologist can speak professionally to Jungian philosophy.
That concept simply seemed absurd and it confirmed to me why I
wanted no part in the profession after that.

24 years ago, I concluded my advanced studies in community and social
development and began work in the same hometown I was born in. I
grew up in a very tumultuous environment, first a run down trailer park,

then federal project housing and later here and there with no long term significance or stability. That wasn't so much an issue as much as not having parents to support me, guide me, or teach me anything really. In fact, my "dad" lived a few miles from me at any given point in my life and I honestly can't recall one word of support or guidance he gave me. I grew up alone, I learned my way through high school alone, and I learned my way through college alone.

25 years ago, I started my profession as a youth crisis counselor. I worked with every local organization in my city at one time or another. I learned the value of really being involved with my clients on a personal level. That is, working with them in their own environment, hence community based counseling. When you help someone adapt to their environment and community, you help them to understand the value of their motive force, their power of will to change the trajectory of their life. A trajectory, keep in mind, that is already going in the wrong direction considering the environment they are born and raised in. People like me were born with the deck stacked against us from day one. But with a little support and guidance, what I learned is that anyone can be, do, or have anything they want in life regardless of the setbacks or obstacles.

10 years ago, I retired from counseling. I had become burned out I guess, maybe suffered a psychological breakdown. I am just not sure what happened. Something in me resigned to a terrible defeat and I simply lost the will to continue. I experienced a very traumatic chain of events that ultimately knocked me down to what was my lowest point in life. I ended up homeless living in a tent in the very city I was born in, my hometown. Could you imagine, raising yourself, rising beyond federal project housing, earning multiple degrees, becoming a counselor working with multiple organizations and 100's of at risk youth only to find yourself homeless and alone? How ironic, considering that is a worse position than how I started in life.

I have never had a drinking problem, drug problem nor have I ever succumbed to vices that often destroy others out of excess, like alcohol did to my biological parents. I hit a mental and emotional roadblock. I didn't know why I was doing anything in my life anymore. In short, I lost myself somewhere along the way on my journey to finding myself. I don't know if I wished for the worst, but I certainly had reached my worst and I was there in the middle of the woods living in a tent. Emotionally broken and mentally lost.

When the dust had settled and it was time to contemplate the direction of my life, at that point, I didn't care how bad my life seemed or how far my fall was, I wanted my life back; I chose to fight for my life and more importantly for my life with my kids in it.

I chose to find myself and fight through whatever emotional and mental confusion I was dealing with and establish who I was again. To find myself had become my life mission. A few years later when I did finally find balance in my life, I decided to work with the homeless and hoped to write about the lessons I learned from my own experiences so that others could learn from my professional background in relation to personal development and how easy it is to reimagine your life regardless of the seeming problems or obstacles that unexpectedly knock you down.

2 years ago I started writing extensively on personal development strategies and created a page on Facebook @PY.powerofyou. All of that work, ironically, is about the way we feel, think, and act and how we use our mind in relation to our emotion while actively following our "dreams." The irony is that I thought I was visualizing for years as I wrote this stuff. That is why this "stuff" is real, because it comes from a part of us that can't access mental senses, an Aphant writes this "stuff". Which means this information comes from the other part of us, the most important part of us; Emotional intelligence.

Emotional intelligence and Mental intelligence, are two widely different concepts. Yes, they are separate from one another. Which means they are separate, though symbiotic, ways to understand and live your life. You lead with one and follow the other, the order of which is up to the individual practitioner.

6 months ago I wrote a book titled Tesla: Interview with a Genius, I write under the pseudonym "Luche ". When I wrote of Tesla and his ability to recall images, it was before I learned of Aphantasia. Only after I reread my writing and came back to that section did I realize he was describing hyperphantasia and how he became a "practicing" aphant. This too was an important discovery. Tesla, the guy is a genius!

5 months ago I woke up and learned I thought I was "visualizing" pictures only to realize I didn't know what I was doing considering all of my family and friends could actually "visualize"

4 months ago I wrote my personal discovery story, you can find an abridged version on Aphantasia.com, they did take liberties with the story but that's okay, you can find the unabridged version within this book and elsewhere on the net. I wrote this story for two reasons. First, I felt compelled to share the shock I experienced and also what I considered important in the aftermath. Second, because I wanted my

kids to read what I experienced when they were ready to read my body of work.

2 months ago I finished the rough draft of my book titled Aphantasia: Blind in the Mind, which I have now included a special reference to Mental Senses based on the polls, statements, and commentary engaged in the facebook group, Aphantasia (non-imager/mental blindness) Awareness Group and also using the statement I provided the group following the initial round of polls.

One week ago, I started actively discussing Aphantasia with the aforementioned group, a group I had been a part of since the morning of my personal discovery. I spent the first 3 months observing. And then I felt ready to ask questions, formulate statements based on those answers in conjunction with the information and description Dr. Zeman provides. I did this to corroborate my writing and to better understand what everyone else thought.

There is nothing scientific about the polls, statements, and commentary of course, but if you think I was waiting another 150 years to start a conversation to define and describe an ability that I can clearly understand, as my daughter explains in vivid detail. Well, that's absurd. No one in the scientific community is trying to define the ability obviously.

Freud, Jung, and Skinner really did have their chance. Of course they knew this information, if they didn't then every word of their work is suspect of being imprecise. That is, I've studied psychology and have read Jung and Skinner in depth, but the way I learned psychological concepts and later counseled the 100 plus youth clients I did, well, that knowledge came from a mirror image of the way everyone in the field was describing and teaching. How do you not talk about mental vision and mental hearing when discussing dissociative identity disorder(originally called multiple personality disorder) Or when reading the book Sybil, the most widely read documented case of a person with the disorder. Why this information is not part of the historical psychological dialogue is mind boggling.

But I can certainly understand why we may have intentionally overlooked something of such profound significance. It could be a really scary book to open. Thinking is second nature, like breathing. Thinking about the way you think, well that is scary for some people let alone the paradigm shift it would cause an entire planet. This affects everyone!.

I appreciate the time I spent observing and sharing in the group. Unfortunately, the administration, moderators and some members later chose to challenge me in an unhealthy way and subsequently led me to release a final statement and self-exile myself from the group.

But before then, the learning and research became an obsession or a hyper-focused activity. I spent the last 2 weeks living in perpetual thought about aphantasia. I would suddenly pop out of sleep at 1 in the morning and be compelled to write a thought or theory. It was a remarkable experience. Unfortunately, no one seemed to be interested in defining the ability only to continue talking about the disability that came with the condition I guess.

If you haven't figured, I write for my kids. My dream is to help my children understand the nature of their spirit in relation to their mind and body. To help them become the best version of themselves. To make sure that they are happy and successful in whatever way that success looks for them. Defining mental senses and talking about the ability or inability with our kids is paramount to any individual understanding.

If you want to change a culture, change the minds of our children, and the best way to do that as it turns out, is to challenge the culture and define an ability instead of focusing on the inability. If we did this, we will learn two things. What we thought was an ability is actually an inability when left uncontrolled and what we thought was an inability is actually the only way we understand the ability, which makes it an important ability.

Thank you so much for reading.

Jeffrey

Introduction

Aphantasia is quite literally a condition that leaves the recipient blind in the mind. It is the inability to generate image and video thought. Even more encompassing, the condition also leaves a person deaf of internal voice and dialogue or having the inability to smell and taste in the mind as well. People can actually see, hear, smell, taste, and touch in their minds?

Well, that's why this was a big deal for me and everyone else that learns in one way or another that they have a condition they never knew existed. Strangely, most people that have this internal ability, also do not know that some people can't and take such a super power for granted. It really is a paradoxical enigma.

I can understand that there are still more species of animals yet to be discovered or that we are learning new things about our own body as microscopic abilities become more modern, like having just found a new body part in the human eye only a couple years ago. But not being able to see images in the mind when 98% of the population can, well that boggles the mind for an explanation. But think about this. People that are visibly blind, that can't see the external world, 98% of them can actually see in their minds too. This is how they can develop spatial recognition. I felt a bit more relaxed knowing this condition was actually more of a benefit for mankind than it was a detriment to me personally.

In fact, after studying the anecdotal information from people that have shared their experience, it has become clear to me that having the ability to see pictures in your mind is a unique ability with many benefits, but there are plenty of negative repercussions to the ability as well. Like for instance, random images that flow through one's mind or the susceptibility to hypnosis or intrusive ads. When you are shopping at the grocery store for instance, could you imagine a picture or ad randomly popping in your head encouraging you to buy one product over another. I finally realized the power of marketing.

Conversely, there are significant benefits to having a condition like Aphantasia. A person with this condition can control their thoughts much more readily. It's sort of like turning on and off a light. We do not have random product placement moments at the grocery store and their only focus when trying to meditate is to feel their connection to the universe rather than trying to prevent their mind from racing from one thought to the next. I always wondered why I couldn't be hypnotized or have never had a headache in my life. For me this answers both questions. That isn't to say all Aphants are alike any more than all people that can see images are alike. It's funny, it made me realize that we all think differently of course yet we all feel emotion the exact same way. A condition like Aphantasia proves both unequivocally.

The biggest question that entered my mind when I personally discovered this condition, a condition that was originally discovered almost 150 years ago, is why doesn't everyone know about this? It is really important to know if a child sees images in their minds. It really is! But even more alarming from my personal perspective? I earned a degree in psychology, worked as a youth counselor for almost 2 decades and I have never heard of this condition of the human mind before. It is clear that some experts believe this condition is biological but others believe it to be pathological, meaning it is some kind of mental block brought on by the person with the condition. Whatever the cause, it matters little, what matters is that as a collective society, we understand that there's a distinct difference in the way our minds work and understanding aphantasia is another step in helping to understand the magnificence of the human mind in relation to the human spirit.

Scientific description

Aphantasia is a condition where one does not possess a functioning mind's eye and cannot voluntarily visualize imagery. The phenomenon was first described by Francis Galton in 1880 but has since remained largely unstudied. Interest in the phenomenon renewed after the publication of a study in 2015 conducted by a team led by Professor Adam Zeman of the University of Exeter, which also coined the term *aphantasia and hyperphantasia.* Research on the condition is scarce. Further studies are planned.

The hyperphantasia and Aphantasia Linear Spectrum

HP = Hyperphant   The exceptional ability to voluntarily visualize very vivid mental images.

P = Phant   The ability to voluntarily recall or create mental images.

A = Aphant   The inability to voluntarily recall or create mental images.

Dr. Zeman and his team coined both terms, Aphantasia and Hyperphantasia in order to best define and describe a person's ability or inability to voluntarily visualize mental images using a spectrum.

History

The phenomenon was first described by Francis Galton in 1880 in a statistical study about mental imagery, describing it as a common phenomenon among his peers. However, it remained largely unstudied until 2005, when Professor Adam Zeman of the University of Exeter was approached by MX, a man who seemed to have lost the ability to visualize after undergoing minor surgery. Following the publication of MX's case in 2010, Zeman was approached by a number of people reporting a lifelong inability to visualise. In 2015, Zeman's team published a paper on what they termed "congenital aphantasia", sparking a renewed interest in the phenomenon now known simply as aphantasia.

In April 2016 Blake Ross, co-creator of Firefox, published an essay describing his own aphantasia and his realization that not everyone experiences it. The essay gained wide circulation on social media and in a variety of news sources.

In May 2018, in collaboration with Zeman, The Aphantasia Network was launched to create a community of people exploring life with Aphantasia, and share stories and strategies to learn more about its impacts.

In April 2019, BBC News published a piece about ex-Pixar chief Ed Catmull and his personal experience with aphantasia, and its surprising prevalence at the company.

In June 2020, Jeffrey Lucero, author and personal development strategist, coined the term Mental Sensory Perception or MSP to better clarify the internal mental ability that most people experience.

Assessment

In the original paper by Professor Adam Zeman, the Vividness of Visual Imagery Questionnaire (VVIQ) is used to evaluate the quality of the mental image of 21 self-diagnosed and self-selected participants. This questionnaire invites the person to visualize a series of images (a relative, a rising sun, a shop they know, etc.) and rank how vivid the image is, from "perfectly clear and lively as real seeing" (5 points) to "no image at all, you only know that you are thinking of the object" (1 point). It is categorized as aphantasia if they score a total of 20 or less across 16 questions.

In the same paper, it was identified that aphantasia characterizes only voluntary visualizations; the aphantasiacs were still able to have involuntary visualizations (i.e. dreams).

Another study posited that frontal engagement driving feedback connections activates sensory representations in the visual cortex; people with aphantasia could have a deficit with these feedback connections such that the visual cortex cannot be activated to produce an image.

Reports of aphantasia may have a psychogenic rather than organic (physical), origin, and it's been suggested that future studies should incorporate psychopathological evaluation

More than a million years ago, one of our ancestors took a walk in the woods and was startled when he or she saw a streak of light come down from the sky and strike the ground. As this individual turned the corner, they saw a bright light consuming the forest. As he or she walked closer to the blinding blaze, they felt their body becoming warmer and warmer until they experienced a stinging sensation. No doubt, they reached out to examine this warmth only to be burned at the touch. At this, they learned to keep their distance but stay just close enough to feel the warmth. Soon, their clansmen and women came running and they all witnessed for the first time the magic of what would later be called fire. It was a discovery that changed the world.

This was one of the first discoveries to change the way humanity lived and the knowledge came from nature herself. The interesting fact about knowledge is that no matter what was discovered in any given year from our earliest years until now, the solution always came from one form of nature or another and it tends to build from one discovery to another too. For instance, when fire was discovered, another person figured out a way to control the fire and still another to transport it until finally someone figured a way to recreate fire. This was all done in a sequential order and often, regardless of the discovery, there was a lineage of individuals involved in the growth of the discovery, because what one person learns and teaches, another is able to grow from and learn something new, hence the development of humanity and the growth of mankind.

Fire, Math, Language, Books, Electricity, Quantum theory, DNA, Penicillin, Periodic Tables, X-Rays this list could go on detailing the singular discoveries in life that have advanced civilization in countless ways. The concept of self discovery is no different. We learn from those before us, on an individual level, we learn from our parents who learned from their parents and theirs and so on. But the real growth of the individual comes internally with the sole expectation that they remain objective in order to learn and grow. Life is an infinite process of observation, experience, and growth.

I discovered Aphantasia similarly to the first person who discovered a way to transport fire. I woke up, had a vision, and realized there would be a great benefit to having the ability to see that vision in my waking mind. The reason this is an important discovery to me as much as fire was to our ancestors, is because I thought about all the reasons this would benefit life and the future of our society, which are many, as

Nikola Tesla clearly describes. So the shock of knowing that most people already have the ability, it was like learning that magic is real and most people possess the power. To put it plainly, it was the most important discovery of my life; it changed me forever.

My Discovery

I woke up on Sunday trying to remember a very vivid dream I just had. It was such a comforting dream and it was unusually clearer than others I've had. I often remember when I dream but I forget them so quickly. I always thought it was strange that I couldn't remember them as soon as I woke up.

This particular morning, I remember thinking how great it would be to see images in our minds when we are awake as we do when we dream. I assumed that's why I forgot my dreams so quickly because I couldn't picture them anymore. I was so excited at the thought, it was a sci-fi discovery; like being able to fly or time travel. Between having the ability to fly or seeing dreams in my waking mind, I would choose the latter, hands down everytime. As my family came downstairs one by one, I shared my newfound idea and one by one they were all confused. Rather, they thought I was confused.

They all said they could already see images in their mind.

"Hahaha...hold on...WHAT?" My thoughts and expressions just went haywire. They were right, I was wicked confused.

Maybe I wasn't clear about my new "discovery."

I needed to understand more fully so I asked them to imagine being a pitcher on a baseball mound (it is the only activity I knew none of them had done before) My step-daughter was reluctant, "I am not picturing something in my mind I would never do in my life" Hmmm. I'm not picturing something in my mind that I would never do in real life? What a revealing impulse response. We will get back to that later.

I pleaded with her to give me 20 seconds of her time and just do it (that's a lifetime to a teenager apparently.) "uhg! fine," she says

My daughter quickly responded with a smirk and said she was on the mound at Fenway and my step-daughter relinquished and said she could see it vividly too but she wasn't at Fenway. And my wife was even more descriptive in what she saw. I mean Fenway was pretty fantastical but she could describe every detail as though she was looking at it. The color of the grass, the force of the wind, the people in the crowd cheering. They all could see one picture or another quite clearly.

I kept repeating dumbfoundedly, "you can see the picture? You can actually see an image?" "Yes, Yes," they responded. "Wait, you can literally see a picture in your mind?" "YES!!!" they insisted.

"Okay, okay," I said, rather somberly. "But I can't."

That was my introduction to the condition I have come to understand as Aphantasia. I googled it for hours and story after story I was amazed at the similarities in my own life. Adam Zeman, Alan Kendle, Blake Ross, their contributions were essential to begin to understand but the many other people who shared their stories were so invaluable and inspirational to me.

My kids would laugh hysterically throughout the day when they saw me reading profusely. In all fairness, I would look up from the computer and tell them with a smile that I was "blind in my mind" or that this was a real "thing."

I am 46 years old. I hold multiple degrees, one of which is a BA in Psychology, have counselled 100's of clients in the past and have written extensively on personal development and the law of attraction. Except, I always thought the ability to visualize and see in the "mind's eye" was a metaphor. Up until this day, I thought it was a figure of speech.

In the aftermath of this profound discovery, there were so many questions. Not just from me but from my family as well. We were all in shock to be honest, although my teenage daughters wouldn't admit it but I know they were.

Seriously, how is it possible that I didn't know most people could actually see pictures in their minds? And let's not even get started on the voices too. But if people could see literal pictures in their mind and I thought I was visualizing pictures, then what the hell was I doing all this time?

I will be honest, for someone that never gets scared, it was at this moment I became a little frightened. I realized the way I thought about my world was completely and undeniably wrong.

But at the very same time, I also realized that everything I felt about my world was still right. It wasn't a shock to my core as I had felt once before in my life. I was still at emotional balance.

Don't get me wrong, I was utterly dumbfounded, but such a revelation made me more happy than any sense of concern I had. Personally, I felt a sense of relief but I am also so happy for the 98% of people that have the ability to see images in their mind's eye. I really am. What a wonderful gift to have.

See, for as long as I can remember, I had been in a perpetual state of confusion. I often wondered why I felt there was something preventing me from rising beyond certain points or I felt obstacles came out of nowhere to hinder my forward progress. I just felt something was missing in my life but I couldn't figure out what it was.

I think back now and remember saying to people closest to me things like, "I feel stuck" or "I feel like I'm in a maze with no lights on and I am trying to find my way." I used to comically portray Al Pacino in Scent of a Woman and say " I'm in the dark here. I can't see nothing Charlie!" That's what my life felt like at times.

How Ironic! Because when I close my eyes, that's all I see. The dark with some specals of light here and there jumping around like protons. But I thought that was what everyone experienced.

Despite the sense of something being profoundly wrong, I always managed to suck it up, dismiss the thought and keep pushing forward. I don't know how to give up on anything, so anytime I felt this sensation enter my life, I would dig deeper, work harder and find a way to make progress despite these seeming setbacks.

My problem was that I always thought you were supposed to see a vision, or an idea was supposed to reveal itself like in the form of a light bulb or something. Speaking of which, I've read Nikola Tesla's writing and how he could see his inventions and even build them in his mind. I mean, he wouldn't even touch a tool until he was finished building in his own mind!

I remember thinking how lucky it must be for people that had an epiphany, a revelation, a flash of genius, or an ability like Tesla's that allowed them to visibly create in their mind. A visual bridge connecting the imagination with reality acting as a roadmap, letting you know you were headed in the right direction. I always waited for this moment to come but it never did.

But this day it dawned on me. The light bulb went on. My mind lit up like a spectacular fireworks display, metaphorically speaking of course. This was literally the revelation I was seeking.

I can't see images in my mind, I can't see the pictures of my kids, or recall the images of important moments in my life, like their births. I can't see the beach, the sunrise or sunset, and I certainly can't see myself pitching on the mound.

Except I can construct the most amazing invisible pictures of all those things and remember in detail how amazing my children's births were. I can create the "pictures", I suspect like someone that can see images, but I can't project them in my mind. I know they are there because I can feel the details of them.

In fact, I have a very strong memory. I can recall conversations I had when I was 10. Sometimes I find myself suddenly embarrassed and feel my face getting red when I have a random thought about something I did decades ago that no one but me would likely ever remember. I can even remember when I had specific thoughts and where I was when I had them. I can recall in minute detail every experience that I have ever had going as far back as 5 years old. The problem is, I just can't see these pictures or images. I can't see the video or hear the audio of these moments.

But I certainly feel the essence of these memories and will never forget them. I recall the data, can formulate and construct ideas using that information, and definitely relive the moments as though they were fresh in my mind today, like they were happening right now.

More importantly, I can create the same sense of detail in the present moment as it relates to building on dreams for my future.

But all this time I was waiting for that "visual" confirmation and all this time, as I now realize, it was my waiting that held me back.

It is the same idea as a blind person feeling their way through the material world. I learned on Sunday that I am blind in the world of the mind and I am more than okay with that.

I know now that I don't need to see the images because I will always be able to construct them and more importantly, I will always feel their essence. And whether you are one of the gifted that can see the mental image or one of the gifted that can construct the data image, everyone of us can feel the image.

Afterall, It is our emotion that connects us to the natural world and it is our emotional connectivity that guides us into our future.

"Whence we are, wheresoever we go, it is only our emotion we bring home."

Nikola Tesla and Aphantasia?

Nikola Tesla was the most brilliant and daring inventor and visionaries throughout history. But what did history overlook? He is the most descriptive case of hyperphantasia ever reported. He described how he would design, build, and test his inventions in his mind. He wouldn't even touch a tool until he was finished building in his own mind!

More remarkably, he was a "practicing" Aphant. He learned, with great effort, to "shut off" the images in his mind. If you want to understand Aphantasia and Hyperphantasia, simply read and understand the process of control Tesla describes.

Excerpt from **Tesla: *Interview with a Genius***, *Luche 2020.
Reprinted with permission.*

There seems to be, at this time, a very popular thought on the ability for a person to create what they want in reality simply by believing in the images in their mind. Do you believe these images help or hinder an individual's forward progress?

A long time ago, when I was a boy, I was afflicted with a singular
trouble, which seems to have been due to an extraordinary excitability
of the retina. It was the appearance of images which, by their
persistence, marred the vision of real objects and interfered with
thought. When a word was said to me, the image of the object which it
designated would appear vividly before my eyes, and many times it was
impossible for me to tell whether the object I saw was real or not.

This caused me great discomfort and anxiety, and I tried hard to free
myself of the spell. But for a long time I tried in vain, and it was not, as
I clearly recollect, until I was about twelve years old that I succeeded
for the first time, by an effort of the will, in banishing an image which
presented itself. My happiness will never be as complete as it was then,
but, unfortunately (as I thought at that time), the old trouble returned,
and with it my anxiety.

Here it was that the observations to which I refer began. I noted,
namely, that whenever the image of an object appeared before my eyes
I had seen something that reminded me of it. In the first instances I
thought this to be purely accidental, but soon I convinced myself that it
was not so. A visual impression, consciously or unconsciously
received, invariably preceded the appearance of the image. Gradually

the desire arose in me to find out, every time, what caused the images to appear, and the satisfaction of this desire soon became a necessity.

The next observation I made was that, just as these images followed as a result of something I had seen, so also the thoughts which I conceived were suggested in like manner. Again, I experienced the same desire to locate the image which caused the thought, and this search for the original visual impression soon grew to be a second nature. My mind became automatic, as it were, and in the course of years of continued, almost unconscious performance, I acquired the ability of locating every time and, as a rule, instantly the visual impression which started the thought. Nor is this all.

It was not long before I was aware that also all my movements were prompted in the same way, and so, searching, observing, and verifying continuously, year by year, I have, by every thought and every act of mine, demonstrated, and do so daily, to my absolute satisfaction that I am an automaton endowed with power of movement, which merely responds to external stimuli beating upon my sense organs, and thinks and acts and moves accordingly. I remember only one or two cases in my life in which I was unable to locate the first impression which prompted a movement or a thought, or even a dream.

Luche

Interview with an Aphant

Wow, I've read your "discovery" story. I found it so interesting that it was literally a story of discovery. You vividly describe the shock you and your family felt. Can you elaborate on that moment?

Well, I can tell you it was a mind bending experience. In fact, I have never experienced anything quite like that moment. I mean, I have had tough moments in life where I got knocked down a few rungs. Once, similar to the wagon metaphor in Edward Bellamy's "Looking Backward", I was knocked down off the ladder altogether. I know full well what it feels like to be shaken to my core. To have my spirit tested. This was different. For me this was a mental challenge not so much one where I had to do any real soul searching to understand what I had just learned. I know some people who also have this condition have different experiences and reactions, but I think the final assessment for most everyone is that it is a different way to process the same information. The single most important question I bet all of us share is "How did I not know until now that this was a real "thing"

Speaking for myself, I felt like for a moment I really did enter that twilight zone where nothing made sense for a few minutes. Particularly, When I told my family about this thought I had, it was funny how the confused expressions traveled between us. First they were confused. You could see the processing slow down for them as they wondered why I was asking what seemed to be a silly question. Then they thought I was joking. Not only am I always referencing psychological and philosophical perceptions and insights but I really never take anything too serious and am often making jokes. So I can understand their hesitation. But when I started asking about the pitcher on the mound and asking them to do that exercise, then they started to realize I was serious.

That look of confusion travelled from them to me like an electrical current and suddenly I was like "WHAT!?" But I really didn't know if it was a question or excitement or both. I mean even now, I will be driving and I will just look out the window in bewilderment. How is it possible that I didn't know this invaluable information? I have read so many personal development books and many psychology books. I have sat in on countless hours of lectures and studied the subject of psychoanalysis extensively. Not one time can I recollect that someone said something about the mind's eye being literal or that some people can't see literal pictures in their minds.

I've even had my own counseling sessions with professional therapists and you would think this would be a primary question to ask at the onset. Do you see literal or figmented pictures in your mind? This may seem like such a simple question but the answer to which is so important. In my assessment, it really is vital to know. Not to diagnose it as a disability or anything like that, but to help the individual understand the difference. If I walked around feeling like I was missing something and just couldn't understand why I felt that way, well that would have made all the difference for me to learn at a younger age.

Maybe that is also true for others. Anyone that "discovers" this condition, will absolutely feel a sense of shock. It is impossible not to be affected in one way or another, positive or negative. Even others that don't have the condition will think the opposite of an aphant; "There are people that can't see images in their minds?" But either way, this sense of shock will follow a positive or negative pulse. It will have a positive or negative effect. Helping people understand, especially our younger generations will make all the difference in helping them develop from that profound revelation.

But it is not just understanding the difference in the way someone thinks but if you want to understand the secrets of the mind, this is the one condition that will reveal many insights in the future. With one study after another we will learn that processing information is very unique from one individual to another. That "failure to communicate" as Paul Newman made famous in Cool Hand Luke, will be a revealing aspect of these studies. More importantly, we will come closer to understanding how our world is in fact invisible and our minds eye brings that fantasy to the screen but those that can't see inside their heads are in fact closer to this invisible source than our counterparts. Learning from this revelation is impactful. Almost as impactful as learning for the first time that you have a condition that you would never fathom to be a possibility just moments before.

When you have heard the words visualize or "picture this" in the past or were asked to practice a visual experiment, do you think back on that moment and wonder why that didn't register in your mind?

I know our brains and bodies adapt to deficiency in ways we cant neccessarily see or understand. Like many people who have this condition, they have spent a considerable amount of time thinking back on any moments where they should have known. But my guess is it's impossible to know something you don't know, can't observe or even read about and since the mind is a private experience I can see how the interpretation would be different. Everyone of us pictured something when asked but just as all voluntary visualizers picture a different elephant when asked, every aphant understands the process of recalling the picture differently too.

My take on that is when we hear the word visualize or instructed to picture something in our minds, we tend to respond in the way that our minds function. That is, if you have never seen pictures in your mind to begin with, then those words would be meaningful in the way you have always conjured a mental picture. I always assumed because the mind was invisible and imagination means to conjure a fantasy well obviously that meant that I just needed to concentrate deeply to "see" a picture that is invisible in my invisible mind. I have run back through my mental history and can't see a single clue where it would have registered. As it turns out, It was a unique type of thought structure that allowed me to adapt to the exercise without knowing I was adapting to begin with.

So when I found out this was a real issue and that I have this condition, I learned then and there that I had a different way to process the image most people can actually visualize. I can "see" all the details of the picture from a past memory or even all the details of a fictitious image I make up, I just can't literally see the picture. That's why it didn't affect me as negatively as I've heard it does other people with this condition. I found it funny that there was such a difference in the way people "visualize" but even more funny that I had this condition. I have written about the law of attraction in detail. My work means so much more to me now that I understand my condition more clearly.

Why do you think it's important to understand and research Aphantasia?

First and foremost, it is important to recognize this as a condition. Especially with our children. We need to know whether they can see pictures in their minds or not as much as we want to know whether they need glasses for corrective sight, if they can see color or any other external sensory condition. I would strenuously argue that it is so important to know whether someone sees images or not; it is vital to helping them grow within our fast paced technology driven modern world.

I am not sure if people "suffer" from such a condition, but I have read reports of people feeling like it impacted their lives in a negative way. It's certainly not a disability from my perspective, it's more of a differbility. Gathering reports of that nature recognizes the importance of understanding at an early age whether children feel different. For example, if a child seems different or withdrawn, this could be a clear indicator why. If they don't practice imaginative playtime and are literal fact seekers at 7 years old, well this is quite a difference in personalities among 2nd graders.

My son is 7 and his imagination is unbelievable. In fact, after discovering I had this condition, I was thinking about my relationship with him primarily. I asked myself questions like how does this affect my relationship with my youngest child as he is at the peak of his imaginative powers. And the truth is it has only impacted one aspect of our relationship from my perspective. I love going to the park with him, swimming is a consistent activity for us and wrestling of course is a staple. I love talking to him and hearing all the wonderful stories he tells from "my brain" as he likes to tell me when I ask him where he came up with that or how he knew this. But the one thing that I realized since that Sunday morning is that it is excruciating for me to play make believe. It has always been a difficult part of our time together and now I know why of course. Make believe is not something I am capable of doing.

So if I was not capable of making believe as a child with this condition, I would bet my behavior was unique, unusual and probably a bit isolating from other kids. I am not sure if that is true, it can be an inaccurate conclusion to suggest because I had this condition at a young age I felt isolated and "different" than other kids. But it certainly would have helped me understand that people literally think differently than others.

It is as important to know whether children have this condition as much as it is important to know whether they are on the ASD spectrum and often people that are on the ASD also have aphantasia. It's precisely that commonality that should be researched and further studied.

You bring up an interesting point. Why do you think it has remained a "Secret" up until now?

Honestly, I am not sure. I am as dumbfounded that this condition exists as I am that this isn't widespread news. My question is, if Galton discovered this phenomenon in 1880, then why would we not have studied this extensively since then. This was the same era when Sigmund Freud became known as the "father of Psychology" although I would prefer this honor go to Carl GustavJung, a more objective, generalized, spiritual and intellectual founding father. But there were many other psychologists who published a wide spectrum of books on psychological thought, including Galton during this same span. Why wouldn't anyone of them reference the pictures in your mind as a relevant discovery?

When you think about the rise of the new age movement, it took shape around the same time as this psychological movement, including when Galton discovered this condition. Wallace Wattles, James Allen and so many others published books on the idea of visualizing and the law attraction in late 1800's and early 1900's. Both the psychological and new age movements slowed but then rose again in mainstream thought in the 40's and 50's this became very popular with Skinner, Rogers, Frankl and the like leading the former and dale carnegie, zig ziglar and countless others for the latter. All these amazing minds, so many published books and not one suggestion besides anyone but Galton that this was a "thing."

I just can't understand how Aphantasia hadn't become more mainstream back then but I am bewildered at how it hasn't in today's technology driven modern age.

I appreciate the connection you made with the New Age thought Movement in relation to psychology. How do you think Aphantasia and the Law of Attraction support one another? I mean, they seem like they are polar opposites.

They are polar opposites in theory. The law of attraction suggests that the best way to visualize your success or that "thing" you want is to consistently and repeatedly "visualize" that thing you want. Well, anyone with aphantasia will tell you, they can't visualize therefore, in theory, they can't use the law of attraction to enrich their lives. But Einstein once said "God does not play chance with the universe" and I think that quote best reflects my point here. It's not the mental picture that is important, it's the ability of the practitioner to understand what they are looking at whether that be an actual image or a figment image. They both matter because regardless of whether you can see it or not, emotion is the primary factor to giving that image relevance.

Visualization has become a major topic in sports lately. The idea that individuals and teams can improve their performance by visualizing speaks volumes as to the power of such a concept. But again, the ability is either a mental or figmented picture, which generally means an Aphant can still "see" the picture even though it's invisible. It is the emotion put into the image that matters most. The majority of aphants report a high level of emotional connectivity to their surroundings and people around them.

Simply put, the Law of Attraction is the ability to attract into our lives whatever we are focusing on but it is the positive or negative emotion we put behind the thing that gives it cosmic mobility. So the mental or figment image is important, neither, I believe, is better or worse, but nothing comes to any person without consistent emotional effort. Some people may see this condition as a hindrance but the truth is our emotion is paramount to any mental activity so in this instance I would see the ability to attract that which we want most an advantage given our ability.

I know many Aphants can feel themselves reeling at their inability to visually recall pictures in their minds, but I can assure you, there are as many benefits as there are seeming limitations. The same goes for people that can see images. It is widely reported that when their mind races, they see image after image and sometimes feel too uncontrollable. When my mind has raced in the past, I find it easy to shut it down and distract my primary thought so other influential thoughts don't intrude. So whether you have the ability or not, there are challenges and obstacles in both instances. For me, just knowing what that feeling was the most memorable sensation. It's the same as discovering a solution to a problem. My mind is finally at rest in that regard to that challenge. Now onto the next...

You went through a very difficult time for a number of years and you referred to this in your life as a "shock to your core" or a "test to your spirit". When you think back at that time in relation to your new discovery, do you see any prevalent insights as to how you would have handled that experience differently?

Well, look, everyone of us goes through tough moments in our lives. We pass it off as life's challenges or tests given to us from the heavens. What doesn't kill us makes us stronger sort of thing. But my take is that we find ourselves in tough situations or even dangerous situations because we put ourselves there. We have specific ailments because we will them on ourselves. Now before you go on a rant, I am not saying everyone wills their own problems, but I am saying 90% of all physical ailments has been scientifically proven to be psychologically based so you do the math. Yes, many of us bring negativity into our lives and even physical ailments. But this obviously isn't always the case. The child with lymphoma isn't willing that into existence, the woman that walked into a Massachusetts deli bathroom and was randomly assaulted or the motorcycle passenger in NH that died when a tree branch fell at just the right moment to hit her but not the driver. These are random acts of life that can't be explained.

Personally, this period in my life I referenced was a critical time for me and I remember seeking out professionals for help and any personal development book I could find, specifically to help me understand why I was feeling and thinking as poorly as I was back then. I was looking for answers to better my life at that point and that's when I came across Rhonda Byrnes "secret" and digging deeper to the source of information Rhonda and all these modern day self help gurus learned from, you travel back more than 150 years bringing you to the 1850's with the works of Emerson, Thoreau, Frost, Wattles, Allen and countless others leading us into the 20th century new thought movement. I have been inspired by each of these writers and many others but I related mostly with Wattles. There was something about the way he described that "intelligent thinking substance" that touched me at the depths of my soul.

I identified mostly with his work and carried his book with me everywhere I went. I even read the book into my mp3 player in order to hear it anytime I could. Despite this effort, I still couldn't understand why it seemed so easy for people to visualize. I am not sure people fully believe in the concept of the law of attraction or law of magnetism, but they should. There is a lot of truth in the process of controlling the fate of your own life by feeling, thinking and doing your best and in that order. But had I known then that I didn't see actual mental pictures like everyone else, well, it would have had a profound effect on how I understood my situation and even many of the books I read.

What I do know for certain is that when you learn you have a condition of the mind that you could have never imagined, it literally makes you rethink your entire life. I wrote that everything I thought about my world was completely and undeniably wrong and that was entirely true. My visuals were never actual visuals, I knew that. I didn't think I was seeing something in my mind that wasn't there. I thought I just wasn't concentrating deeply enough, that was it, my inability was not focusing enough. And when I started to realize I could "see" images, I knew that they weren't there but I could see them as much as I could feel them. They were always invisible.

So, I don't know why this isn't a common concept in the minds of everyone. It really affects everyone, people with and without the ability. For example, I was having a conversation with my daughter the other day. She was telling me about when she went to Fenway for some kind of ice skating exhibition or contest a couple years ago. I said "oh, they put ice rinks on the field", a bit surprised. She responded, "no, it was like a ski jump or something like that" I then tried to understand the picture she was trying to describe because it didn't make any sense. "A ski lift made of ice?" Imagine seeing someone skate down something like that? Right, it didn't make sense.

But she started getting annoyed that I didn't understand. I responded, "I am sorry I can't understand the picture you're trying to tell me, I am not sure if you know but I have a condition that doesn't allow me to visualize pictures and what your describing doesn't sound like anything I ever heard of." But this was a perfect example of how arguments seemed to present themselves in my life. Most arguments arise out of miscommunication primarily but a conversation between a visualizer and an aphant, well that is actually comparing the proverbial apples to oranges.

I really find it fascinating that you thought of this concept coming out of a dream state. How important do you think dreams are?
I think dreams are awesome. Whether you dream in pictures or figments, I think when you're sleeping it matters little. In fact, I really think I dream in pictures but I don't fully trust any aspect of my mind at this point. The dreams seem like pictures, but what if in this sleep state, my mind is forming "pictures" in the same way it always has but because I am unconscious, it appears like images. We just don't know enough about this condition to know anything for certain. I know it has been reported that some Aphants don't dream at all so I can't speak to this outlying faction either but since most people with this condition can dream, it makes sense that the memory of these dreams are hard to recall. I know I have about 30 seconds and then my dreams become obsolete.

But in terms of meanings and symbolisms of dreams, I have learned since finding out that I don't see actual pictures so it is up to me to make sense of my "images" as much as it is up to me to decipher my feelings during waking life. One of the exercises I do is what I call thought surfing and is no different than free writing, a technique writers do to pull out ideas, connections and random thoughts on paper. Thought surfing serves the same purpose except it's a lot like dreaming. Before I learned about this condition, it made sense that this exercise would help to understand my thought process. But since then, I realize people that can see the image can thought surf so much more effectively. Either way though, understanding the thoughts regardless of their presentation is a reality based exercise because it is happening right now and therefore can aid an Aphants understanding as much as a non-aphant.

We have all read stories, watched movies and learned of suggestions that we are living in a dream state. The movie Inception is a perfect example of this point. It is not really possible to know if we are living in a dream within a dream within a dream like a hall of mirrors but in my opinion, it doesn't matter because regardless of the condition one person has or a disability another has my job is to be a good father, loving spouse and contributing member of the society I live in but mostly, I want to live my best life everyday and that requires a positive focus and outlook for my future. Since the future is a dream state, then I guess every moment we are alive, we are on the doorstep of our dreams.

You described the moment you found out your whole family could see images. What about before then, as you were waking up, when you thought of this as a new discovery; how did your emotional state respond?

I think that was the primary reason for the shock and awe I felt. I really thought I was onto something. I don't even like watching or reading sci-fi, they tend to require too much imaginative thought but I love stories about time travel, that is the one exception. So when I thought about seeing pictures, I was excited at the new thought. Well it was new to me. I have never heard of this idea, never seen it in movies bridging the topic and so I explored the concept in my thoughts. Given the option to fly or see images, yeah of course I would choose images over flying anytime. But this brought me to an interesting point. Everyone would choose the ability to time travel over flying or mental imagery any day of the week I think but between flying and mental images, as fun as flying might be, actually seeing your thoughts is invaluable to personal development.

If you want to make any change in your life, you would have to think about that "change" first. As an Aphant, that means thinking through that process of course, but having the ability to see images, well all you would have to do is think through the process once and then recall the image constantly thereafter. As an Aphant, we would have to constantly think of the idea and try to conjure up the invisible image but that takes far more mental power than just voluntarily visualizing. Think of it this way, it takes 10 hours to read a book but an hour and a half to watch the movie. That is the difference between seeing mental images and not seeing them.

 But once you understand the image, whether metal or figment, the more constant and consistent this image recall is, the quicker you will get to where you want to be in your life. Change happens the moment you wish for change, but it takes shape the more consistent your actions are. But no action takes form before your thoughts. That is, we have to think about what we want first, whether that is a cup of coffee or a million dollars. How many times have you gotten up from the couch, went into the kitchen and then decided to get that coffee. No, you think about that coffee first and then take action.

So the discovery for me was really inspiring. And I would suspect when someone finds out they don't see images, the process from that point is a lot like my question "what the hell was I doing all this time?" The answer was that my discovery was pure and since I had already developed the ability to "see" invisible pictures then the next best thing for me was to actually see those pictures. Again, I know not all Aphantastics understand this process the same way so I can't speak to how others must have felt about discovering this truth, but for me it was perfect timing in my life.

So you didn't have a hard time accepting that you were lacking an ability that most people have?

No, not at all. I know it was shocking in the moment but as I reverse engineered my life, I realized that I understood what I had learned to do, which was to adapt. But I did so without knowing I was adapting. My initial explanation to my children was to imagine living in an isolated jungle and everyone had just one arm but the village thrived, buildings and homes were built and nothing really prevented the growth of the community. Now imagine coming across another village for the first time and realizing everyone had two arms. It would be a two part process; first, you'd experience shock and awe, then realize that everything you did in your life up until that moment would have been twice as easy if you had two arms. That's exactly how I felt.

It is easy to get into the mindset of "what if" but that only matters when you made a mistake in the past or perfecting a skill set. "What if" is the same as asking yourself "what would I have done differently if I were to repeat that scenario?" or "what can I do better?" This thought process is important for bettering your life. And this is also a process you can control and use to make change. But being disheartened because you didn't have an ability that you learned other people have well that's limited thinking. That's like having the ability to play basketball and being jealous every time you watched a game on TV because they were professionals and you weren't. That mind doesn't do anything but push you deeper into a perpetual state of sadness, or worse, a bitter perspective on your reality.

To put it in general terms, there is a process when dealing with any emotional state, especially negative states and similar to the 5 step process of grieving, acceptance is the most important. You can not achieve anything beyond your current state of being unless you accept your ability for what it is. When people lose a limb, they are initially in shock, then awe and may feel disheartened for having lost something they once had but anyone that ever got over any traumatic situations in their lives, whether it happened voluntarily or by accident, they learned to accept that it happened first and then adapted second. It does not work in reverse. Lao Tzu said it best *"Life is a series of natural and spontaneous changes. Don't resist them; that only creates sorrow. Let reality be reality. Let things flow naturally forward in whatever way they like."*

In terms of acceptance. Do you think the online groups help or hinder people who have this condition?

They certainly help, especially in the beginning stages of learning about and understanding this condition. The Aphantasia Network is a phenomenal first step in the process. I think the work they are doing is very important. They bring a well structured form of thought around the subject. And the online forums are helpful as well but they can also be limiting in some ways. So I definitely think it can hinder your forward progress as one enters a new phase of their life which of course is living with the knowledge that you process information slightly differently than most people. But this process is no different than someone on the ASD spectrum or who lives with Aspergers. It is just a different approach to the same thing we all share, which is living this life of ours.

But the only real hindrance as I see it is that when people come together to discuss their similarities in relation to their shared disability, they tend to grasp onto the notion that they are different and go down that rabbit whole which often leads to more confusion or even setting you up for failure. When reading these forums, I see a lot of superficial questions and even more dramatic responses like "I know we all can't remember things clearly", or "Since we've had our visualization taken from us" or any other question that groups everyone together is never helpful in understanding our personalized response to the condition. Of course we are all trying to find answers to important questions we have but the truth is whatever limitations an aphant has you will find someone with voluntary visualization with the same limitations. My friend for instance can see mental pictures better than anyone I've asked so far but she has a very weak memory, I can't see mental pictures but I have a very strong memory, so there really is no correlation whatsoever for many of these traits people are asking about.

That doesn't mean they are not important questions to ask, but we should ask the right questions, be careful about over generalizing the condition and provide honest thoughtful feedback that will help provide a deeper understanding and thereby lead to a more collective approach to growing our knowledge base while helping each one of us that is now learning to live more fully with this condition.

That brings up an interesting point. You mentioned that you were so happy about the other 98% who could see mental pictures. Tell me about that.

As I mentioned earlier, the difference between seeing mental or figment pictures is really in the ability to visualize your thoughts. Of course when you see mental pictures you are literally visualizing your thoughts. When I think of a dog I hear barking outside, I think of a dog barking outside. I do not try to think where the dog is in relation to where I hear the barking, I do not care to wonder what type of dog it is or whether it is on a leash or not. On the other hand, I have heard reports that when people hear that same dog barking they immediately visualize the type of dog, where it is and whether it is in fact on a leash or not. This is your thoughts in visual form. Obviously your visual may not be accurate but it gives you a reality based idea. That is an amazing ability to have. And I am so happy that most people can visualize their thoughts, It really is a wonderful gift to have.

And the reason I say it's a gift is because it allows you to literally see the options you have for your life. When I was doing research on the condition originally, I googled a lot of different key words and read a variety of stories. Interestingly, I started seeing stories related to aphantasia pop up in my news feeds, the diabolical spying algorithm I suspect. But I read a fascinating story Jeff Bezos shared on how he made the decision to quit his lucrative job on wall street, give up a big bonus by leaving mid year, move to the West coast and start an online company from scratch. How did he make such a big decision? He mentally pictured himself as an 80 year old man and thought about how he would feel if he left his job and the big bonus and then asking himself how he would feel if he failed in his efforts to create this company he had envisioned in his mind. His take away was that he never remembered the bonus or the significance of his job or whether he was successful or not in this new business venture, he would have felt worse had he regretted not following his dreams. Your thoughts are your dreams and the images are the visual representation of those dreams.

The sad truth is that most people do not realize what a gift they have and likely you would only see it is a gift and not take it for granted if you never had it and learned that other people did or if it was taken away by some freak accident like being afflicted with a major head injury. When you don't have an ability you wish you had it, and when you do have it, you tend to fail to see the significance of it. But to have the ability to see mental pictures and conjure insight, like Bezos explains in his story, well that really can make all the difference in your choice to move forward. Visual confirmation is critical. It's letting you know that it is working for you. Conversely, visual reflection can also help people see the dangers and pitfalls that may be lurking around the corner. Mostly, it confirms what you are thinking with visual identification.

The most important lesson I learned was that I always had the confirmation I was seeking and that little voice in the depths of my soul always told me it was there, "right in front of you" a mantra I heard over and over in that silent voice, but I just didn't understand that until I learned the truth. It was right in front of me because it was invisible and I couldn't see it. People that can see the images, well it comes a little easier and a little more clear because it's in the form of a repetitive image and perhaps, the voice too.

You brought up Nikola Tesla in the same sentence as you did epiphanies, revelations and flash of genius. What relevance does Tesla have in relation to Aphantasia?
I have been a huge admirer of Teslas for a while and read most of his written work. It was only a few months ago I came across one he wrote about harnessing the energy from the sun. It seemed unique but as I read the beginning pages I realized that this particular book was one

focused on human development. I think Tesla is the most important active genius the world has ever seen so to hear what he thought of human and personal development, well, he was spot on from my perspective. And if you read his history, he certainly was arrogant, which I believe was his ultimate downfall, but he also had self esteem issues, addiction issues and generally was emotionally and psychologically unbalanced at various times throughout his life too. He was a human being, complete with all of human folly and he overcame those follies.

But perhaps the most important thing to know about Tesla is that he was not an Aphantasic. He had a great imagination and even clearer ability to construct mental imaging in his mind, perhaps more than any other documented case. As I mentioned, he explained in detail that he wouldn't start building his inventions until he was finished constructing them in his mind. He even went on to explain that he would even test his contraptions and when he felt he had refined them to the point of perfection, he would then get to work on the literal project.

This process is so important for people that have the ability to construct in their mind of course. Perhaps we all don't have the mental strength of Tesla, but we all have a level of mental strength. If you do have the ability to create mental imagery in your mind, use this to your advantage, practice and strengthen this gift. You may not change the world but you will change your own world in so many amazing ways if you learned to trust the images you create and discard the ones that deter your dreams and visions for your future.

With that said, if you do not have this ability, you have an even more amazing one. You have the ability to construct invisible pictures in your mind, which I believe is an even greater strength. You are still capable of constructing the most amazing dreams and visions for your future, but you just can't see them. I bet, if you "look" close enough, you will realize that you feel every detail. I know I can and since learning that I too was an Aphantastic, I realized that the only skill I had yet to develop and the one issue that I truly felt held me back, was not trusting the unknown, the unseen figments of my imagination. And now that I have, I know everything and anything is possible whether you have the ability of mental imagery or an even stronger ability as an Aphant.

That reminds me of the exchange you had with your step-daughter. I found her response to your request to picture a pitcher rather revealing.

You are absolutely right. In fact, I think that the entire struggle an individual has in understanding their own powers of creating the life they want, the entire crux of the self help and law of attraction movement in general is in that one simple statement "I am not picturing something in my mind that I would never do in life" That was an off the cuff involuntary response from her and it was so revealing that one only need to understand the significance of such a statement. It means everything.

Think about it. The entire personal development concept, whether you're talking about spiritual, psychological or any other motivational perspective, relies on the individual envisioning what they want to improve in their lives and then imagining how that would be better. Whether you can actually see pictures or not doesn't matter because you can still think about what you want and work towards that. Now, if you have the ability to construct mental imagery it is certainly easier for you to see your thoughts in image form, but regardless of how you "picture" in your mind, it will always come true. Beware or be aware what you wish for because it will always come true is no longer a figure of speech it is actually the immediate truth of your thought process.

A lot of people report trouble getting negative memories out of their minds. Or when their minds start racing it's because they are perplexed with a particular issue. I can see how this is perhaps one way mental imagery can be a disadvantage. If you are able to shut down the negative and focus on the positive you will be amazed at how effective your mind starts to work in your favor. Conversely, if you never imagine in your mind what you want for yourself, or you learn to think original content, ie, picture in your mind what you have never done in your life, you will start to see how thinking outside your own box can have amazing benefits.

On the flip side of that argument, if we constantly focus on the negative in our lives, then you are in fact picturing things in your mind that you don't want in your life and are doing the exact opposite of what you actually intend and this inherently impedes your personal development or worse, it brings together the exact opposite of what you want for your life. Remember, every single thing you do or receive or create in your life you have thought about it in one way or another and this is true of what you think about consciously and of course what you think about subconsciously. You may have heard the saying "in the absence of good leadership, people will follow anyone" well, in the absence of a conscious effort, you leave your subconscious in charge, and generally, that is never a good thing because you will conjure up fears and doubt far more when you are not manning the ship so to speak.

If you realize that everything you do in your life has been thought of in your mind first, you will always "picture" things in your mind that you intend to do in your life.

So, when you were "waiting" do you feel like you wasted years of your life just "waiting"?
Everything, and I mean every moment you are aware of your own experiences, you are learning. Each of these moments is a teachable moment and we should recognize the lessons available to our senses. Often, we tend to allow life to flash by and wake up from time to time wondering where the years went. The truth is that even if you are always living in the "now" you will still wake up 10 years from now wondering where the years went. This is because time is an illusion, life is eternal, movement is the process, and "now" is rooted in a perpetual movement.

The sun and the air are the two most important components of our life, together they form the existence of Water, the most important sustenance of life. Without the sun or air, water would not exist and without water, life can not exist. But the most important aspect of each of these properties is that none of them remain still, they are in a constant state of transition. We are made up entirely of hydrogen and oxygen and therefore share the same qualities as our sun, air and water. We are part of this amazing movement. Even more amazing though is that water has memory, retains and responds to emotion stimuli and can forge mighty paths with a steady and consistent effort.

So to answer the question directly, "waiting" is an exercise of doing nothing and while it seemed like I was waiting all this time, the lesson turned out to be the action I was always taking. That is, as I "waited" for my moment to come, I was always doing and always adapting to the moment that I know now would never have come. I was never going to get that clear and undeniable epiphany because I was expecting something to come in a certain form and that form was not possible based on my physical abilities. But the more I focused with absolute intent, I learned to be more patient, more resilient and especially more determined to find the answer I was looking for. My answer came that morning, which could have been bittersweet, but because I always remained optimistic despite the harrowing struggles, I also always managed to find a different way to carry on.

The answer that came, the missing piece to my puzzle was that I am not capable of seeing the form I expected to see and because I didn't know of this inability, I adapted. I found my own way, which I suspect everyone with the condition has found one way or another. I think that's why my immediate reaction was one of relief. I found the answer I was looking for probably because I stopped looking and suddenly the answer rose above to my thinking surface when I was most able to sense the lesson being revealed.

I definitely understand the anti-climatic nature of your "discovery," and I know it will continue to be a library of lessons to sort through. As of this moment, what is the primary takeaway for you so far?

Our emotion is paramount to everything else we know about life. Our bodies are subservient to our thinking and our thinking is subservient to our emotion. The irony is that I have written extensively on the concept of having a trilateral balance between your body, mind and spirit. In fact, if you look close enough at the details that make up our lives, you can see how this trilateral balance makes up the entire universe in the form of substance, movement and order or as Tesla put it, energy, vibration, and consistency. Even though you can't see energy anymore than you can see light, it is clear that energy is the invisible body that connects everything, vibration is the movement that gives rise to form and consistency is the eternal nature of Life.

People generally think that we have a library of emotions but the truth is that we simply are emotion and there are points on the circular movement of such emotion that gives rise to what we perceive as different emotions but they are all simply different forms coming from the same source. Think of your emotion like you would the ocean. Waves rise and fall due to external factors, but they will always return to its natural balance when the external factor gives way. This is true of emotional response as well. We generally give rise to hate, love, anger, sadness when we are affected by an external stimuli but no emotional state can give rise for too long; happiness subsides as does anger and every other emotional state and what you are left with, is your true state of balance. When you understand this constant movement, you will understand your own strength of patience.

When I discovered that I had this condition, I was perplexed because if people actually see pictures, and I thought I was visualizing, then what the hell was I doing? It turns out, what I was doing was making the invisible picture clearer in my invisible thought process. In fact, these invisible pictures became so clear based on my ability to meditate and focus, that I actually assumed this is what it meant to visualize. So I had adapted so intimately to the practice of visualizing that the invisible pictures became real and the only way I could see them was to feel them using my emotion. If my pictures were real because I could feel the essence, that could only mean that the essence is also a major aspect of the practice of mental imagery as well. While it is great to be able to see our thoughts in picture form, it is more important to feel them regardless of their form.

So when you mentioned that you felt like you were in a maze with no lights on, is this what you were referring too?

Exactly. I was referencing the feeling. But the interesting thing about this particular feeling was that I didn't know why I was feeling it at all. I mean, we are all on an individual journey right, so as we continue on our journey, we are always seeking out one answer or another, even if we don't consciously recognize this process, it is inherent within our DNA, our own essence. We want answers. And I am a constant seeker of this truth. Perhaps to the point where I am preoccupied with finding "the answer" in as much as an athlete feels the drive to become the best at their respective sport. My "sport" is finding the answer to life and I am obsessed with this discovery.

So it would always puzzle me and at times become infuriating when I ran up against a wall or I felt like I was repeating a cycle that would reveal itself in ways that seemed mystifying. If you ever saw the movie Groundhog Day, this is a good idea of the process I speak of. When we live our life in a perpetual cycle, we often don't realize we are in the middle of a cyclical or episode until we have concluded the cycle, recognize our mistake and then strangely repeat the process but with different sets of variables.

The "wall" or "maze" is nothing more than our own creation and the way to our own happiness is a direct line to who we are right now. All this time I was searching from something that wasn't even real and the "feeling" I constantly had that I was in a maze with no lights on trying to find my way, well that was the answer I was seeking. And the answer for me is that there are no lights, there is no maze and we will perpetually seek to understand the nature of life from this moment. And you you suddenly find yourself in a moment of enlightenment you will quickly realize that there is more to learn and hence you set forth for the need to understand from a deeper level. But no matter how high you go in the process of personal awareness, there is always a higher point still. We think we look out at the expanse of a mountain range and can see everything at once, but the truth is you really can see anything, it is simply your mind putting the image together like a big panoramic picture. Try looking at anything at all and you will realize there is always a smaller point to see. The maze is not a construct but rather a process and the center is a figment of the imagination.

Not to limit the extent of your point as it relates to Aphantasia, but many people feel the same sense of feeling lost whether they can mentally produce pictures or not.

Well, I am sure that's true. But my description of feeling lost was a metaphor in describing my personal experience. I would not suggest we all deal with the same struggles or perceptions in life, that would be absurd. But the one thing we all experience the same in this life is our emotional connection to the world we have been born into. We all look different, we all think differently, but we all feel in the exact same way. Love feels the same for you as it does for me. Anger feels the same for you as it does for me. Sadness, happiness and every other emotional expression feels the same for you as it does for me. We are connected by our emotional significance and the more we understand the depth of our emotional connections, the more clear life becomes.

When we take a step back and reflect on how we feel in certain experiences, we will realize that it is this emotional response that determines the effect of that experience. For example, there are three people working at the same counter at the local coffee shop. The customer is angry at the order and starts berating the staff. One staff member reflects back that anger and expresses a similar sense of disgust toward the customer. Another staff member becomes nervous and in turn anxious and can barely keep himself from shaking because he has become so emotional. The third staff member shows to be indifferent to the customer, tries to understand the problem and then develops a solution irregardless of whether the customer is satisfied or not.

The customer is irrelevant to the situation. It is our response to the situation that is the only relevance to your life. How you feel in response to another is simply a stimuli/response relationship. When you realize that you are both the stimuli and response, you will find yourself in the same sense of balance as a wave in the ocean. We follow what we feel and if someone or something affects that journey, we either let it impede us or we push past the stimuli so that our response to our own lives continues unimpeded. The more we practice this effort, the easier our life becomes and the more steady the journey.

So you're absolutely right. Regardless of whether you are an aphant or not, the process to personal discovery starts and ends with your emotional connection to the world you live in and has little to do with a maze of course.

You mentioned earlier that you understand now that those revelations or epiphanies you were seeking will never come. What did you mean by that?

Well, I didn't mean that they will never come, I just meant the way in which they would come for me is different than how they would be revealed by someone that can see those mental images. The most profound realization for me was that I was always right in the direction I was going. The ideas that would come to me, always came in the silence and blackness of the backdrop even though I was always waiting for the mental image to reveal itself. This is what I thought the light bulb moment looked like. The invisible picture would flash in the form of a real picture. I just didn't think they were constant pictures.

I would often say that you can't trust your own mind, because there is a part of your mind that will tell you you're wrong or that you're not good enough or you can't do it. This is self defeating prophecy. If your own mind is telling you this, then how could you trust it to steer you in the right direction when you need that guidance the most. The answer is simple. You can't trust your own mind. You have to remember your mind is a tool and you have to both develop the tool and then utilize it the way you need it. This is the same as suggesting you are both an observer and active participant in your own life. It is easy to see what you must do when taking a step back but when you are in the middle of your life, it is difficult to see those steps. That's precisely why we need to take time for reflection every day, so we can stay focused on what is important for us on our journey.

The answers we seek will always come to us but instead of looking for or thinking we know how they will come we must follow the wisdom of the great ancients when they told us to see without seeing, prepare but do not plan, or seek but do not search. When we learn to trust our inner guidance, we will quickly learn that we are not smart enough to see the "how" things happen in our lives and we certainly are not privy to the "when" things will take physical shape. That is, we can prepare to meet the person of our dreams, but we can never plan for who they would be. We can see our future life in our dreams, but we can't actually see the details in real form. When we learn to seek without searching, we will better prepare for our future by allowing the unknown to reveal itself in due course of our lives.

"Whence we are, wheresoever we go, it is only our emotion that we bring home." Can you explain the significance of this last sentence in your story of discovery?

I once wrote a quote I called "Imagine" It was calling the reader to reflect on the qualities they think would be helpful when imagining themselves going to a utopian society. What qualities would you bring?

truth, happiness, resilience, gratitude ext. The point is, whatever you would bring should be integrated in your life now and if you mature while developing these qualities and many others, then you will become closer to the emotional epicenter of all of life. And whether you believe in an afterlife or not, the truth is, it can't be a physical formation since everything living dies here on earth.

So any sense of afterlife would have to be centered on emotional intelligence. That is, if we live beyond life on earth, if life is truly eternal, as every religion and spiritual movement on earth believes, then our eternal life consists of eternal energy and since emotion is the root source of our living life, it would have to be the only expression that we consist of when we transition from this world. Therefore, our emotional intelligence is made up of and developed by the qualities we deem most important in our lives right now. Our emotional DNA is our eternal life so it is up to each one of us to develop and strengthen our emotional awareness. This is our awareness of being and this is how we become the truest form of ourselves in this world and the next.

Regardless of whether you are an aphant or not, when you truly understand the nature of your feelings in relation to the image or figment, you will understand the value of your emotional state and realize, on a deeper level, that everything around us is connected by emotion (energy in motion), and whatever answers we seek, they will be found in the emotional significance of the experience.

Mental Sensory Perception

Defining the Hyperphantasia

and HypoAphantasia Spectrum

with special reference to Mental Senses

...Mental Sensations of the Physical Senses...

This summary was only possible with the many members who answered the polls and participated in what were some very lively discussions in the private facebook group *Aphantasia (Non-Imager / Mental Blindness) Awareness Group*. If anyone reads through the historical commentary, the answers came from everyone that answered the poll, questioned the integrity of the subject matter, and read the process of understanding the subject.

In the two previous polls:

93% of respondents answered yes, having mental vision is describing the same ability as seeing mental pictures.

93% of respondents answered yes that the statement below is an acceptable statement regarding aphantasia while including the other mental senses.

Aphantasia is the inability to voluntarily visualize mental images. Some people with Aphantasia are also unable to voluntarily hear mental sound, smell mental scent or odor, taste mental flavor, or feel mental touch.

Some people are unable to recall or create one or more of the mental senses.

Most people are able to recall or create one or more of the mental senses.

Mental Senses are the mental sensations of the physical senses that are recalled or created in the mind.

Mental Sensory Perception is the ability to voluntarily recall or create mental sensations of the physical senses in the mind.

This is how we talk about Aphantasia and the other inabilities regarding mental senses.

More importantly, this is how we ask our children if they can see, hear, smell, taste or touch in their mind. It is important to know this information at an early age.

This information is not considered scientific by any scientists or "neuroscientists working in the field", but it will be as we start the conversation about why these abilities are not even observed, discussed, or studied. In fact, they are clearly overlooked for some reason. They are just in their infancy, yet, they have been known as one inability not five years ago, but for almost 150 years. I'm sure, Dr. Zeman would agree that it is important to widen the scope of mental senses and to the importance of studying all of the inabilities along with their mirrored abilities.

We observe the subject, then we talk about the subject, then we study the subject, then we define the subject, then develop scientific answers to understand the subject. There is no other way to learn and grow. That's how Dr. Zeman and his team coined the term Aphantasia. And that's what we did in the group!

Talking about an inability without defining and including the ability in the conversation is difficult. Talking about 5 separate inabilities that are clearly related to our physical senses, well that's easy, you define the ability.

To the people in Aphantasia land. Thank you for allowing me to be a member of the group. I learned a lot and had a number of thoughtful and insightful conversations.

Memory

Memory is important but only for the end user and the detail in which they choose to recall. In the simplest terms, memory is a 3 part system; Encode, Store and Retrieve. We all encode a moment in time to our memory, this is inevitable and an organic experience, but even if there were 20 people experiencing the same moment, the encoded experience would be different for each individual. Perspective, focus, emotional significance and many other parts of the experience determines what details of the information gets coded and what doesn't. Think of it like watching a movie and reading the news at the same time. You could certainly get the jist of the movie and probably look up when a major moment occurs, but the fluff parts, the parts that connect the main storyline are pretty much lost on you because the news, i.e. reading, takes precedent. Conversely, you absolutely could not get the jist of a news article if you watched a movie and skimmed the paper, it is not possible. Those with Aphantasia are readers. The information is there for all, but with the inability to see internal images, the aphant is still left with the most important part of the information, the manual.

Now looking back at the 20 people sharing the same experience, encoding works the same way. Each of us encodes life from the perspective we are seeing it from, but we all encode the experience. And we all store this information whether we consciously realize it or not. But it is the retrieval part of our memory that is the bigger mystery and the one part that some experience greater success than others. For instance, when a friend brings up a memory of an experience you both recall, it usually is quite different than your own, even though you shared the same moment.

Fortunately, they are your memories. But to be more reflective, when we remember anything, we also sense the emotion that is inherently attached with the moment. Whether you see pictures in your mind or not, whatever you intend for recall has an emotional component to the memory and this is often the reason many of us do not have strong memories. We tend to forget why we stored the memory to begin with, or we choose not to relive the emotional component, which is significantly more powerful than the actual image. But to be clear, even many individuals that can see pictures in their minds, also report poor memory skills so it is not an issue that is directly related to Aphantasia. But there are a few tactics that anyone can utilize to better retrieve these memories.

Focus

Simply put, focus involves the ability to pay attention to things that you are doing at this moment. Focus helps to avoid distractions that may cause mistakes or accidents. It simply allows you to be more fully involved in the details of the experience, the importance of the moment. Whether you are at work, with your family or having a conversation with a friend, your focus determines the information that is encoded and stored and allows for the retrieval of that information more readily than if you tried to do two things at once or were not fully involved in the moment. We live in a modern era where many of us are literally addicted to our phones. The phone is the newspaper , in the aforementioned example, which means you are living your life half in and half out of focus and subsequently lose information, in most cases, vital information from the moment.

Neuroplasticity, the ability of the brain to constantly reform, reorganize and forge new growth, is a vital component to memory, specifically retrieval of encoded and stored memory. If you truly want to make any change to your mental state, intended focus is paramount to anything else you could do. Intended focus is another way of saying there must be purpose behind your intentions. But this is also true for memory as well. If there isn't an emotional component to memory, then there isn't a need to recall the memory and the only true way to attach emotional significance, is to be 100% involved in the moment.

Structure and organize

I generally like to think I am a good partner in my shared household. I do my share of domesticated responsibilities and obligations and I do try to be a better spouse than I was the day before. But there is a real key difference between me and my spouse. I am very fact oriented, which is a key characteristic many aphantastics share. I prefer everything neat and in order. I structure my areas very neatly and keep things free from clutter. I have found by doing this, I am more able to focus on the tasks at hand rather than being overwhelmed with distractions.

When I go grocery shopping, I don't need lists because I systematically go through the aisles and get pretty much everything I got last week with a few additions here and there based on different menus I have in mind. But the real obstacle comes when my wife asks me to get "a few" things. These seemingly minor additions tend to take me an extra 30 minutes at the grocery store. This is the quintessential stick in the spoke. Considering I am generally in and out of the grocery store in 20 minutes, these 3 or 4 "minor" additions force me to walk back and forth through the store 3 or 4 times because I can't find the items; they are not part of my pre structured routines.

We have to be aware of life's constant surprises. Moments that shake us out of our directed thinking or generalized way of doing things but make no mistake, habits and routines are vital to making consistent tasks mindless. Habits and routines are important, in fact, some would argue, especially James Clear and Charles Duhigg, they are vital to establishing lifelong positive changes starting with little baby steps. But from that first baby step becomes a habit, then routine, onto a consistent action sequence, which is your life Journey, and ultimately your destiny.

Rehearsal

Replaying a moment in our minds, whether in pictures or figments, after you experience it is a key reason why some of us have stronger memories and others do not. The more we rehearse the more parts of the moment we remember and the more ingrained the memory. Studying for a test is a perfect example. The difference is the short term and long term retention. Often when we study for a short term experience, we tend to forget most of the information a short time afterward. But if it were a critical component to your personal development, you would replay that information in your mind so much that you were practically obsessed with the retention part. Because whatever you obsessively retain in memory in the very moments after your experience, retrieval will be significantly easier and practically immediate. Any expert in their respective fields is passionate and studies their profession with purpose, therefore, the information is never lost, only rehearsed time and time again until it becomes ingrained as inherent knowledge.

To be clear, it is just as important to rehearse these moments before we experience them as well. It seems imaginative and a bit fantastical, which is a trait many apahants don't prefer, but rehearsing in figment thought is as important as someone that can rehearse in pictures. It makes the intended experience easier and in many cases, more successful. We have all heard stories of how athletes play markedly better when they visualize playing before stepping on the field. Imaginative rehearsal makes all the difference and should be practiced daily.

Journal (one moment at a time)

I personally do not like keeping a journal, but I think about every detail of my experiences on a regular basis and even mid points throughout my day I will recap, so to speak, parts of these moments that were important or noteworthy. This is what is called a running memory journal. I suspect if I could visualize actual pictures, this process would be easier but it's a process I utilize and have perfected over time and the more I utilize my ability to keep this running journal, the easier it will be for me to recall memories and moments later.

Some of us need to actually write these moments down and review them later. There are great benefits to keeping a journal and if your memory is weak compared to how you would prefer it to work for you, then keeping a journal is paramount to making this happen for you. Remember, anything that helps the ability for you to recall a memory is important for you today, but more significant for your future.

Draw a visual

Patti Dobrowolski is the leading advocate for the importance of drawing your life the way you see it and more importantly the way you want it to be. I have written extensively on the ideas of magnetism and the law of attraction but I was always most fond of the picture drawing that Patti describes in length. There is something magical in the way she talks about how the picture changes your entire emotional focus the moment you put an idea to paper, similar to the way a journal works for people.

Simply put, using a sheet of paper horizontally, draw two pictures. On the left, how you see your life right now. And on the other side, draw how you want your life to be in a year from now. The year is arbitrary, because life changes sometimes much quicker or longer depending on one's dedication to the change. But by doing this project, you are conjuring emotional significance. In most cases, the colors on the left side are not as vibrant as those on the right. Because you are using the powers of imaginative appreciation and gratitude to will that and often, this process is completely unconscious.

Emotional balance

As a general rule, we remember emotionally charged events better than boring ones. In fact, the latest research suggests that it is the emotions aroused, not the personal significance of the event, that makes such events easier to remember.

An investigation of autobiographical memories found that positive memories contained more sensorial and contextual details than neutral or negative memories (which didn't significantly differ from each other in this regard). This was true regardless of an individual's personal coping styles.

The memory of strong emotional moments and events may be at the expense of other information though. Thus, you may be less likely to remember information if it is followed by something that is strongly emotional. This effect appears to be stronger for women.

It does seem that memories are treated differently depending on whether they are associated with pleasant emotions or unpleasant ones, and that this general rule appears to be affected by age and other individual factors. Specifically, pleasant emotions appear to fade more slowly from our memory than unpleasant emotions, but among those with mild depression, unpleasant and pleasant emotions tend to fade evenly, while older adults seem to regulate their emotions better than younger people, and may encode less information that is negative.

Pennywise

The easiest way to understand Pennywise is simply take pennies from your birth year to the present. Put these pennies in a cloth bag or jar or something where you can reach in and grab one without readily seeing the year. When you choose a penny, look at the year on the penny and think about something significant that happened that year, write it down and then put the penny back.

You will notice two things start to happen. First, memory recall is so much easier when you associate it with seemingly random exercise such as a penny grab. And second, your memory is not only intact, but one memory from 1995 will create a chain of memorable reactions leading to new memories from the same year. Specific dates are not important. The year acts as a catalyst to conjure important memories for that year.

Memory recall may not be immediate, but your brain will find a way to reveal what mattered most that year. As you write down these memories, you will quickly fill a journal with amazing recall experiences. Keep in mind, that negative memories are as important for recall as positive ones. Remember, you're not reliving your past by recalling these memories, your learning from and using this information to build a better future perspective.

Equations & Percentages
People that can't see images in their minds are generally regarded as literal thinkers lacking imagination, it should be comforting to know that following a mathematical equation can be very mind & life

altering; Science is the basis of life, but math is the universal language of life. Utilizing math, specifically equations for various aspects of life, helps anyone see the end result before action is even taken. Sort of like seeing a picture in the mind before actually experiencing the moment. We know $2 + 2 = 4$ as much as we know $10 \times 10 = 100$, these are facts. Equations are fact and the more we can factualize our actions and intended results, the easier our life becomes.

Pi, the Fibonacci sequence, and the general concept of the number 3 are critical components to all of life on this earth and throughout the universe. The origin and meaning of which is as much a mystery as the human species, but while understanding the sequence and relationships of these numbers may not reveal the meaning of life, it will undoubtedly reveal the way of life. A direction or road map that will make this life easier. Science and math tend to do this for us, make life easier if we commit to the nature of discovery and subsequently, invention. For our purposes, there are 3 primary building components to personal success as Thomas Jefferson so eloquently pointed out; Health, Wealth and your personal pursuit of Happiness (Personal Growth).

Health

Your health is essential to your physical well being, but it is also very important to the development of your Spirit and Mind. This is not to suggest you have to be in top physical shape or even exercise daily. But you do have to care for your body in a way that promotes positive growth and maturity, just as you would a freshly planted seed. With the proper nourishment and attention, your body will reflect the state of your internal wellbeing.

There are two major detractors in the realm of modern society which threaten the very natural process of physical development: television and processed foods. Western society specifically has become inundated with both. If they are not consumed with realistic observation and wisdom, then these will essentially allow negative growth to create the resistance to the positive growth that actually comes natural to your development. Newborn babies are precious precisely because they are at the purest form of human development. How they are nourished from the moment they are brought into this world determines the future health of that child.

If you considered your own body as precious as the newborn baby, it is unlikely you would drive up to any fast food restaurant even once in your life, no matter how enticing the fries or burgers are. You would care for your body with the same sense of purity as that of a newborn. Yet ironically, as children grow from the toddler years, it becomes almost a rite of passage that they visit a McDonald's regularly. The draw to these establishments is not necessarily lazy or even poor parenting, it is that the concept of feeding our children a few nuggets and fries is considered "okay" by societal standards, when the truth is that it is never okay to allow anyone, let alone children, to consume foods which we know are harmful to our natural physical development.

The social standard to healthy living is quickly eroding, because the social acceptance of negative food consumption is being altered with the wide spread promotion and blatant false advertising that "junk" food is the norm. To thwart the ongoing slew of such messages, you must individually recognize the importance of when and why you consume a particular food. You know the moment you decide what you want to eat that it is either good or bad for you, yet we tend to ignore our own thoughts and accept the immediate physical pleasure of the food, rather than realize the negativity of its future consequences.

Television entertainment is exactly the same in this regard. One only needs to surf the many channels and see the absurd and ridiculous shows that are promoted heavily, and you will get a sense of the decay in moral and ethical standards. As Carl Jung emphasized, the collective consciousness is best reflected in the mainstream attention to the details. If millions of people are watching shows such as Jersey Shore or real housewives of somewhere, what is being suggested about the health of our collective consciousness? We are collectively being manipulated to believe, quite nonchalantly, that such programming is only entertainment, and without harm in any regard.

But in truth, what you watch and eat are the two most prevalent aspects of yourself that reflect the intentions of your internal development. This is not to suggest that entertainment or all foods are bad, but to point out that moderate consideration to the healthy development of your body is of primary importance. Understanding what you are eating is important to any diet. Understanding what you are watching is important to understanding your psychological connection to your internal interests.

In order to live a completely healthy life, you have to begin making decisions on what to eat and watch based on the natural emotional state based on your interests, rather than simply doing what is easy. That is, we often put our entire lives on autopilot, rarely knowing with certainty why we do most things these days. If you are to find a balanced model for healthy living, you must be conscious of what you consume and what you are doing for entertainment; both are key components of a healthy lifestyle.

The hardest part about sticking to a plan of action is staying focused on the plan. The mind can be a tricky aspect of personal change because it will always try to convince you to take the path of least resistance, even though the mind's path is only based on passivity regardless of the consequences. That is, of course it would be more enjoyable to sit on the couch and watch T.V. than to run 3 miles every day. In fact, your mind is quick to entice your body to follow suit. But in order to develop a solid healthy long term lifestyle, you must establish an emotional charge to outweigh your mental laziness in order to force your body to follow the proper natural plan for change. This is precisely why you must remain active in thought at all times.

One of the easiest achievements to reach is also one the hardest challenges most people deal with on a daily basis. But remember that it is your mind that makes this a difficult endeavor. Trust your emotions, follow their lead, and your mind will have all the strength you will continuously need in order to shape your physical world into the healthy living you envision for yourself.

Weight loss and exercise is a billion dollar industry and it seems every 3 months there is a new diet that is going to revolutionize the way we lose weight. The kato and gluten free, the atkins and vegan free, it doesn't matter what the diet is or what the next one will be, and there will be another one. The truth behind any and all diets is based on the statistical certainty that if you eat more calories than your body requires, you will gain weight in proportion to the extra calories. Conversely, if you eat less calories than your body requires, you will lose weight in proportion to the lesser calories. You will lose weight based on this proportional concept alone. The package is the diet program and at the core of any diet program; reducing and/or burning calories.

For instance, the average 40 year old moderately active man needs 2500 calories a day to maintain his current body weight. That means if he eats 2500 calories everyday while continuing to be moderately active, he will neither gain nor lose weight. Since 3500 calories is equal to the loss or gain of one pound of body weight, this means that if you followed the equations below, you are guaranteed to lose weight. You could eat 2500 calories of chocolate cake everyday and still lose weight. And that is true of all foods or any combination of foods you eat.

Follow these mathematical rules and you will see real results within the first week.

8 x 16 circulation rule

Drink a gallon of water everyday; 128 ounces. 8 ounces 16 times throughout the day or any variation thereof then choose any equation below. Water speeds up metabolism, it cleanses your body, curbs appetite, and generally makes you feel better. Keep in mind that soda and fruit drinks have calories so include this caloric intake in the rules below.

25% expenditure rule

$$Y25\%(7) + X(100)(7) = Z \text{ calories}/3500$$

Y = Calorie intake

X= Mile

Z = Calories consumed and burned

Eat 25% less daily caloric needs and walk, run or crawl one or more miles daily and the result is the number of pounds you will lose in one week. A more rigorous exercise routine increases the results proportionately but simply walking everyday will produce the exact same results in due time.

For every mile you walk, run or crawl, it really doesn't matter how fast or slow you go, you will burn 100 calories on average per every mile gone. If you walked 5 miles today, you are using 500 calories to get there. If you eat 500 less calories and walk 5 miles, you have a net loss of 1000 calories today. In 7 days, that is 7000 calories or 2lbs. The recommended weekly loss rate. That is not a coincidence. Because eating 500 less calories is hardly a difficult diet, the hardest part is becoming a calorie counter; knowing how many calories you intake everytime you ingest food or drink. And the even tougher challenge is establishing the consistency in your daily routine to make these small yet powerful changes.

And the best part of this process is that you don't and shouldn't think about your weight again. Simply follow the math and the results will speak for themselves.

3X ingestion rule
(8-9, 12-1, 5-6) 500 + 500 + 1000

Eat your meals only between the allotted times provided and never eat a single piece of food outside the 3 windows of edibility. The last meal you ate digests within 12 to 15 hours so if you stop eating at 6 and don't eat again until 8, you will give your stomach a rest, which in turn will decrease in size, making you feel full with smaller portions because your stomach can no longer hold the same amount of food you had been conditioning it to hold.

As a general rule we should eat 500 calories for breakfast, 500 for lunch, and 1000 for dinner. You don't need snacks, because you can survive on any one of these meals, you certainly don't need all 3, but more energy equals more productivity so eat your 3 squares a day if you prefer.

Intermittent fasting rule

(12-6)

Skipping breakfast and eating just lunch and dinner or even having 3 meals in this 6 hour window also makes life easier for you. If you condition yourself to refuse food outside the allotted window of consumption, or condition your body to wait for the next meal, you will be able to immediately control one aspect of overeating.

The second aspect is keeping your calorie intake under the 25% threshold. But again, with practice, you will condition your body to listen to and follow the rules you have established for yourself. In time, you won't feel even the slightest sense of hunger because of this consistent conditioning.

Sure experts will tell you that skipping a meal is bad for your health but an equal amount of experts will tell you the opposite. Sure, experts say dieting leads to zero sum weight loss, but an equal number of experts say otherwise. This isn't a lose weight quick book, follow these simple equations and you will see real results.

Increase cardio or weight exercise and you will see better results quicker. But the one fundamental truth is, if you don't balance your caloric intake, you will never see the results you're looking for or at best, you won't be able to track the results without knowing how many calories you intake vs how many you are exerting.

Wealth

A few years ago, at a time I now consider to be the point where my life was shifting towards a darker, more destructive path, I remember getting a fortune cookie that said something like my well was about to run dry and only then will I know the true value of wealth. And while I always entertained fortunes, this one hit me the moment I read it. Though similar to my perspective at the time, I shrugged it off as nonsense, and arrogantly continued forward with my destructive perspective. But I recall now how the value of wealth means significantly more than just money. In fact, money is but a small fraction of true wealth, yet as a society, wealth and money seem to be synonymous.

If you truly want to become a stronger successful individual, you must remember that wealth is the accumulation of your entire life experience as it pertains to you. If you are to live a completely successful life, it must reflect the interests and ambitions you truly feel. It must include the career or job you wish to pursue. It must include family and friends you truly want to be with and have healthy relationships with. It must include the hobbies and interests you actively pursue. And most of all, it must contain a steady emotional balance that is rooted in growth and productivity. There must always be movement and growth in order for your life to be great.

Wealth therefore is the steady growth and development of your life in the direction you intend to go based on the dreams you wish to follow. When one is truly wealthy, they are able to recognize that their physical world is an exact representation of their internal emotion and thoughts. That their world has become exactly what they have envisioned and the path of least resistance becomes the more dominant course of travel. The more smooth your days, the more closely your internal and external worlds mesh.

A person has true wealth when their physical world reflects the deep commitment and passion of their internal development. When you are honoring the best of you and taking steady consistent steps toward positive growth and personal development, you are building wealth in every way. As you reflect on the ideal image of your life, you are concentrating your attention on the value of the things you create within your life. Whether this is money, relationships or your health, you are creating more wealth the more you adhere to your ideal self-image.

And as you maintain steady progress, you are building more and more wealth for your life. And true wealth, like energy, will never go away. It will always strengthen the foundation for which you continue to grow from. This is precisely why the true value in life has little to do with money because as your perspective centers on the invaluable aspects of life, your ultimate success will be pure.

Therefore, in order to focus on the invaluable, it is easier to use a model that guarantees the safeguard of the societal value of money. Following the mathematical certainty of managing your money is as easy as following your caloric intake and expenditure, it simply requires an initial dedicated effort and then the process becomes seamless from there.

40% expense rule
Not including food or personal expenditures such as coffee or ice cream cones, budget your household expenses so that you are not paying any more than 40% on household expenses which includes house payment, utilities, vehicles and insurance ect. If you keep these expenses under 40% you will establish a household focused on financial balance, which is necessary when planning for a healthy financial future. There is no guessing in math, the answer is always going to be the answer so if you want to consistently be on the right side of that answer. Set a budget, adhere to the budget and most importantly, be objective because math isn't personal and neither should your personal financial goals.

20% investment rule

Once you set a budget for household expenses, set an investment budget. What goals do you have for your future investment? How much money will it require? Whether this is your first house or an apartment building or business, any of these investments require money and in order to raise the money, it should come from your own pocket. Warren Buffett is the financial genius of geniuses. He says don't borrow money once your credit is in good standing...so follow this advice religiously...don't borrow money.

After the 40% is deducted from your monthly income, next take out 20% for your investment interests. This fund should be transferred to a seperate account so that it can remain untouched until your financial goals are realized. It doesn't matter if this is $50 a week or $200 a week, once you set the investment rule, keep it simple, respect the rule. Similar to caloric intake, do not deviate. Follow the math, it doesn't lie, but it certainly adds up quicker than you may realize. If you put $50 a week aside for a year, that is $2600. If you left it untouched, in 5 years it will be $20,000. Enough to get going. If you put aside $200 a week, that's $10500 your first year, maybe even enough to get started too.

15% vacation rule

If you budget for vacations as a necessary component as you do your investments and household strategy, you will get into the routine of saving for your next big vacation. Take out 15% of that household income and put it into a vacation fund. This guarantees you save a little more than $8K a year. Enough to take two week long vacations anywhere. But keep in mind, if you are frugal like me, you will spend half this and use the other half for monthly weekend excursions. That will keep the vacation alive all year long!

15% retirement rule

Simple. Take 15% and put it into a retirement fund. Think of this money as though you were having a conversation with your older self. You owe this to that person. We tend to overthink things and money is the easiest of all. What you do today matters tomorrow more than it matters today. Put the 15% aside and don't consider what ifs...that's what your will is for. So once you divvy up all these wealth related focus points, make sure your next move is creating a will so that you can take care of the what ifs that may happen.

These wealth related items give you a general idea of the importance of budgeting your money more wisely. Unlike shooting darts in the dark, it is better to see what is happening to your money by using easy to read, easy to track math. Math doesn't lie. And since I am a literal person, perhaps because of my condition, this math helps manage my life a whole lot easier. Also, think of each of these savings as an expense, a priority that you must adhere to, as much as paying insurance or your electric bill. When you pay yourself first, you will absolutely reap the benefits later. Oh, and what you have left, the last 15%? That's what you use for groceries, gas for the car and a night or two out on the town. Don't worry though, following the personal development equations below will help you increase your household income with the same sort of absolutism as paying yourself for vacations and investments.

Personal Growth

Your pursuit of happiness or personal growth is the most subjective aspect of yourself but it is also easily measurable. Contrary to popular belief though, this must be and in fact can only be measured by yourself. It is easy for others to look on and say you should do this or that, as easy as it would be for you to say the same to someone else. But the truth is, only you know what it feels like to grow and since you are the base product and the expected growth product, you need to measure yourself from where you are and base that on where you want to be. Even though personal growth is seemingly polar opposite to any mathematical equation you could think of, you can still apply a statistical equation to this area and it will provide you with measurable personal growth.

$$E = A(P + T + F)$$

Unlike equations for health and wealth, personal growth is a completely subjective experience and there is literally just one way to formulate and measure personal growth. First, you start with a baseline and this should typically be measured by how you perceive your skill level now and comparing that to how you perceive it in 2 weeks, one month and then 3 month increments measured indefinitely.

E = Expert

Whatever you choose to do, whether professional or personal in nature, should be done with the intention of being an expert. Expert status, according to Malcom Galdwell and many other academics, is achieved when you accumulate 10,000 hours dedicated to any area of knowledge or activity. A medical license in the United States for example is only provided to a recipient if they have studied for 10,000 hours but also worked in their field of medical study for an additional 5,000 to 10,000 hours on average. We qualify doctors as experts when they have exceeded the 10,000 hour mark.

Pretty much any activity will reveal the point of impact to be 2,000 hours a year for 5 years to become an expert in your field of interest, which is why a leader in a field of experts is always older, wiser and committed to years and years of service. Most of the powerful politicians in Washington didn't get there overnight. In fact, it was years and years of cultivation. An expert amongst experts requires dedicated time, attention and longevity; there is no other substitute for success than committing yourself to being an expert in whatever you do on a daily basis and in multiple areas of focus. You can cut corners all you want throughout life, but like Karma, those corners will come back to cut you too.

A = Activity

Everyone should strive to be an expert in every aspect of their life. An expert spouse, and expert parent, and expert coworker ect. Aside from being an expert at an actual skill, we can obviously become experts in other less acknowledged areas. If you watch too much tv, become an expert in reading. If you tend to be lazy or procrastinate, become an expert in reverse engineering this process to becoming an active doer. As though impulse is more immediate than repulse.

When we narrow our day down to activities we perform and recognize not only why we do these activities but what they mean to our collective well being, we will begin to see how each moment really is a building block of our greater good. We either advance from moment to moment or we backtrack, we are either gaining ground, or losing ground, and this "fight" is generally always internal.

We all work on various activities on any given day. It is easiest to recognize each that we participate in and become an expert at each. This is the point where we will see momentous value in our lives. The engine revs, starts moving and then gains momentum...in our life though, it is infinite momentum.

P = Performance level

How much effort you put into your activity directly determines the level of success you achieve. There is no substitute for effort. It is easy to do anything half ass, but if your goal is to become an expert, slowly define the level of importance the activity means to you. I am not always a fan of the tortoises methods, but when it comes to performance level, slow and steady is important. Obviously it doesn't feel that way in the beginning, as you see the rabbits racing by, but as you build strength and commitment, your level of success will gain the momentum needed to surpass all of your expectations and suddenly, you are the leader in your own race, running circles around the closest competitor, all without even being competitive. Hmmmm...imagine that!

T = Time

Time is an illusion, if it even exists at all. Existentialism aside, the time we put into the activity should be focused on the time you have in a single day. Focus on tomorrow when it comes. The sun rises and sets today so do all you can with an eye on tomorrow, but with a full commitment to today. That 1000 mile journey really does start with a single step, and the next that follows. The more sure footed the first and second, and so on, the better you pace and longevity.

When we break our expectations down to taking things "one day at a time," we are literally centered on this moment. From this perspective we really can accomplish anything because you are no longer focused on the end result. Some activities can be determined with time but personal growth and success, there is no destination so the time you put in is accumulative yet doesn't reach any level of completion. That is, there is no limit to the capacity that experience of an activity accumulates. It's similar to the search for enlightenment. Every point of self discovery leads to another point to discover. There is no end, just a deeper, more intimate understanding.

Time is only important as it relates to right now and the consistency of your effort to reach your goals.

F = Focus

Most people are trying to juggle many things at once during their workday – so how does focus help? Focused concentration is central to productivity and success, even when "multitasking". Except you only think you're doing more than one thing at once. Research shows that the brain really only processes one cognitive task at a time. You're time-slicing. So your ability to focus on each one, and not be distracted from it unless and until you choose to change focus, is critical.

Why does focus matter so much? I'll put out three main reasons: Productivity, clarity of thoughts, and safety.

1. Productivity

    For me, this was a major difference. When I'd been practicing mindfulness daily for a year or so, I started to notice that I was getting far more done. I'd been doing the same type of work for many years, and I had standard estimates of how long it would take me to do various things. Suddenly, I did not need that much time to do anything. Focus was only part of the reason – my ability to be fully present in each moment, rather than over-thinking the future and fretting about what might go wrong also contributed.

2. Clarity of thought

Being able to focus also has made it easier to think clearly. When I choose to stay focused on one thing, it becomes clearer to me. It's as if processing all of the factors and possibilities has time to "stew" in my brain. The relationships, concepts, and priorities seem more obvious and crisper as that stewing process proceeds. I'm also better able to see when I don't have the clarity to take action with confidence.

No one can focus continuously, but Daniel Goleman calls this fewer conceptual gaps. In the September 28 Harvard Business Review article "Mindfulness isn't the Answer to Everything. Here's When it Helps" he gives an example of the mind wandering during a meeting. Gaps in focus lead to gaps in understanding.

3. Safety

Having spent my career in personal development, safety is top of mind. Front-line workers in many industries must stay focused on their environment or risk injury to themselves or others. Concentration especially while performing repetitive tasks is not easy, but can truly impact health and safety.

For me, it has been more about psychological safety. Being able to focus on what's really true in the present moment has allowed many of my fears for the future to dissolve. So this aspect of safety also contributes to clarity and productivity.

Focus practice

Ironically, practicing focus does not involve thinking directly at all It's about mindfulness, which is noticing mostly sensory perceptions in the present moment. Modern brain science highlights that mindfulness strengthens the prefrontal cortex, which is our center for thinking and cognition. It also diminishes the power of the primitive amygdala that triggers fight or flight and other strong emotions.

Try these sample practices to strengthen your focus

- Follow your breath in and out for a few minutes (Goleman and others point to 10 minutes, but even 1 or 2 minutes can help. When you notice your mind wander, gently pull it back to the breath without judgment.
- Notice just one part of your body, like your hands for a few minutes. See if you can sense fine differences between each finger or each section of your palm. Just be with it.

These are not quick overnight fixes. Practice consistently every day for at least 21 days, and see whether you notice any difference. If you think you might, continue it for longer and see what happens.

Wheel of Life

The Wheel of Life is a simple yet powerful tool that helps you visualize all the important areas of your life at once. It is often used by life coaches and career coaches to give their clients a "bird's eye" view of their lives. By looking at a visual representation of all the areas of your life at once, the wheel helps you to better understand which of your life areas are flourishing and which ones need the most work. And this is precisely how you subjectively measure your life so that you have an objective representation of the direction your life is going. More importantly, using this tool allows you to separate the areas you feel need attention from the ones that are spot on. Although, as you use the tool consistently, you will find that the areas change quite often.

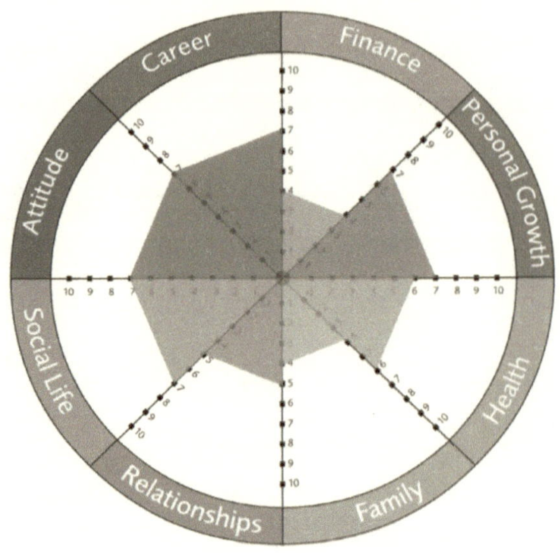

Life is an effort to maintain balance so it is only natural that as we balance one area, another becomes slightly unbalanced requiring the participant to refocus on an area that was once flourishing. But as you master the art of balancing multiple areas, the effort to maintain a steady rhythm becomes part of your natural ability, like breathing.

The Wheel of Life is a way to take a good, hard look at each facet of your life, and rate its relative quality level, so you can uncover which areas need more attention than others. Consider each area like a spoke of a wheel: When one of the spokes is shorter than the others, it can throw the whole thing off balance. By getting this "helicopter" view of your life, you can identify where you are excelling and where there is room for improvement – to discover where the gaps are between where you are today and where you want to be.

There are countless sites, pages, apps and examples on how to use and assess yourself with the Wheel of Life but here is the real secret they all share in common. You simply have to rate on a scale of 1 to 10 how effective each area is, keep track of your assessment week by week. And most important, be honest in assessing yourself. It is precisely like a math problem, it will always be accurate if you can use the tool with personal objectivity.

Another important concept to keep in mind, that while you will see some areas are of your life are lacking and you will feel an immediate need to make change even though you may not even know how to effectively create change, it will serve the participant well to simply think and imagine what and why you feel this area of your life is not balanced. Like magic, the answers seem to come easier when we spend less time focused on the problem and more time simply thinking about possible solutions. For every one problem, there are a dozen solutions at least. Let your imagination run wild, whether you can see pictures in your mind or not, we all have the ability to sense the solutions we need for our lives, we just need to practice the patience to take them one step at a time.

Original Thought Form

Every decision, action, or consequence is based on a single thought. Like every great idea, discovery or invention in this life, the original thought is formed from an assimilation of nature. That is, man came up with the idea to fly by watching the birds soar above; computers were developed from assimilating our very own brains. Our thought is as much a part of nature as everything we see around us, yet we often overlook such an idea because of our complete and full immersion in society. We rarely have time to think for ourselves, let alone think about every thought we have, and the thoughts that stem from them. Life becomes as confusing as trying to find the center of a target while standing in the middle of a house of mirrors.

While the idea of thought forms into a massive and complex system of thinking and it is almost impossible to understand its origin, the truth is, you do not need to over complicate your life and you certainly do not need to think of where thoughts come, or why the next thought follows the first. Life would be exhausting if it was conducted in this way. You do not have to know the theory of thought, any more than you need to know how your body knows to breathe; it just does.

Similarly, just knowing the theory of thought exists allows you to appreciate thought in its purest sense.

However, you do need to nourish your thoughts like you should nourish your body. The more healthy your personal outlook on life, the better position you are to experience healthy and happy thoughts. If you choose to eat fast food and chips, your body is less impressed with you than if you ate healthy, and your body will likely let you know just how unpleasant the experience was.

Thought works under the guidelines of this process as well. The happier and healthier your thought, the better situated you will be for the next thought. It is very difficult to always maintain a happy and healthy outlook in life in order to protect your future thoughts, but luckily, your thought is not so fragile as to collapse the moment a negative element enters your life. The more positive experiences you have and the more positive the engagements you have, the happier and healthier your thoughts will be, and the easier it is to deal with the potentially negative situations that will inevitably arise.

It is important to remember that one of the trickier aspects in life: while everything is happening in the moment, change always seems to be a future event. But this is an illusion. Change occurs the moment you determine change to exist. If you wanted a glass of water, this thought is realized the moment the thought occurred; the result followed a process leading to the end experience. Every other thought follows this same methodology. Thought becomes a series of thoughts fueled by the energy of momentum. And the speed of momentum is dependent on the intention of your action based on the original thought.

Intending to get a drink is hardly a complicated task, so the speed of momentum is in effect significantly faster because your intent of thought is relatively uninterrupted. The more significant the thought, the more impressive the seeming obstacles or interruptions seem, but if we think of every thought and future action as simply as we do of getting a drink, then our intent is as free as a balloon floating in the sky, uninterrupted and unhindered.

Two people working at the same job with the same skill set and same responsibilities should, within reason, have the same experiences and productivity. Yet it is our thought and intended action that makes a world of difference in the productivity of the day. Likewise, a person with an Ivy League education and a high school dropout are not different on the playing field of life when we take into account the thought process of deciding the course for our lives. Dave Thomas, the founder of Wendy's, one of the largest privately owned largest fast food chains in the world, was a high school dropout; yet he had many of the best-Ivy league educated people working for his company. How you cultivate thought is an individual concept. No one can develop your thoughts for you, any more than they can control your physical movements. Likewise, only you are capable of staying centered on the primary thought of action. If you want to reach your ultimate potential in anything you do, then remember that your intentions must be solely based on your thought, commitment of action, and the sequence of events to follow, all with the purpose of leading to your thought's eventual reality.

Since we know that thought is a process leading to action, it is important to be committed to the thoughts we keep. Our life is bombarded with information in every moment of everyday, and our brain takes in every aspect it can see, hear, and sense – all of it, from every direction at every moment. But how we process that multitude of information is a completely individualistic endeavor.

Thought is as magical as the mystery of life itself, and being able to think this thought through leads us to a quagmire. This quagmire is, itself, the very reason we overlook the most important element of our life. Nevertheless, by merely knowing the theory of thought exists, we may allow ourselves to determine that the positive or negative experiences we accumulate throughout our life can be added to or detracted from the moment we choose to better our life. And we may better our life simply by bettering our thoughts.

Positive and Negative thought

Virtually every living aspect of life is based on the concept of positive and negative charges. In nearly all circumstances, both a positive and negative charge is needed to make life move. Since our thoughts are based within the life form, then the positive and negative combination applies here as well. Good vs. bad, beauty vs. ugly, strong vs. weak; this dichotomy is inherent in our being, since obviously we are very familiar with such opposing points of view. Knowing both, though, does not mean practicing both. In order for thought to exist, it does need a strong base. And since the base needs stability, it also needs to know the opposing point of what the base stands for (or against). For instance, just as a negative charge for a battery serves the only purpose of grounding the positive charge, our negative thoughts should also work within this functionality. Knowing a negative thought and practicing that thought are not the same, any more than it is the same to know how to rob a bank and to follow through with the action of doing so.

Throughout each day, as is typical of the human experience, we have a series of negative thoughts. It is virtually impossible not to have a negative thought. The most important idea, then, is that our positive thoughts outweigh the negative ones, and that the positive thought is fueled by the desire to make a reality based on the image of positivity. Whatever you need in your life is supported by the original thought, and branches from there to subsequent thoughts which lead to the realization of that thought. This ultimate thought, positive or negative, will becomes a reality over time, depending on the consistency of your adherence to the original thought.

Once you understand the nature of thought as a single individual form specific to you and your personal development, it is easy to see how that form is connected to the larger invisible realm encompassing all of life. Like a flower sprouting from the form of an individual seed, thought branches from the individuality of a single thought to form into the reality of the action thought.

Active and passive thought

Active and passive thought are two distinct and opposing processes of thought. While the thought form is equally specific and relative in the moment, our intent of form is altogether different, and determines the growth of the thought form. When we think of a thought in the passive sense, the intent to make thought a reality is wholly dependent on one's drive to make that thought a reality. If you only think that you want a glass of water and have no intent to receive it, then that simply becomes a passive example of what you could have. It establishes no desire to follow the subsequent thoughts that might make that first thought a tangible reality. Like every other individual thought form, there can be no final experience without progressive thought to lead that charge.

The passive thought can be exceptionally forceful and persistent; it is simply beyond the control of our conscious wills, if we allow this to be true. Seemingly out of nowhere, thoughts will enter our minds: memories, fantasies, inspirations, dreams, songs we get stuck in our heads, lists of things we need to do, and so on -- often accompanied by intense, even compelling, emotion. These passive thoughts are sometimes false beliefs about ourselves or our realities: I am a failure, I am amazing, life is hopeless, all you need is something, and so forth –

an unrelenting and unending flood of different impressions, desires, beliefs, emotions, and judgments, to name a few.

When these thoughts enter our minds, there can be a natural tendency to accept them, either as reality, or as whom we are, and to engage our active minds with them to a greater degree. We tend to react to these thoughts as though they are reality itself, as opposed to being reflective of some more subtle level of reality. We can then spend inordinate time and energy trying to draw these thoughts to some conclusion, or else following them blindly. In such pursuit, we frequently are led away from the deeper significance that these thoughts convey, and find ourselves in a repetitive process of self-doubt, guilt, confusion, and disempowerment. And all this time, we are unable to grasp the deeper significance of the thought as it pertains to active thought.

A mind without awareness of the difference between active and passive thought is vulnerable to believing that thoughts are who we are, and that all thoughts are created equal. We can become so accustomed to staying within our thoughts, active or passive, that it can be hard to see beyond them, and difficult to make effective change. We are not fated, however, to remaining in this daunting, constrained conundrum.

We have an ability to engage our thought process differently, as opposed simply being at the whims of those thoughts, images, feelings, fantasies, and sensations that present themselves.

Wallace Wattles is one of the most effective writers regarding the thought process in relation to the Universal Intelligence. He vividly declares that what you think about, regardless of the physical representations in your current life, is true. He claims that the more you imagine the truth of those thoughts transpiring, the quicker and more effective your reality will be in allowing this thought to be produced. The toughest challenge you have to contend with is the notion that you can create your ideal life when you realize that your thoughts produce them based on emotional balance.

Through a process of cultivating mindfulness and playful imaging, figment or literal images, we begin to discern the boundaries between active and passive thought, and understand the significance of each. Consequently, we may find greater peace and balance. This, in turn, enables us to more fully to engage both our inner landscapes and outer worlds with greater awareness and clarity, and become more conscious within the various stages of our journey.

Conscious and Subconscious thought

The conscious mind is the part of your mind that is responsible for logic and reasoning. If you were asked about the sum of one plus one, it's your conscious mind that is going to be used to make that addition. The conscious mind also controls all your intent of action while being conscious. For example, when you decide to make any voluntary action -- like moving your hand or leg -- it is done by the conscious mind. So whenever you are aware of the thing you are doing, you can be confident that you are doing it by your conscious mind. If there is a cup of coffee beside you, and you decide to take a sip, then all of this process will be done by your conscious mind, because you were 100% conscious while doing it.

The conscious mind is also known to be the gatekeeper for the mind itself. If someone tried to present you with a belief that doesn't match your belief system, then your conscious mind would absorb and adjust this belief, and then either discard or assimilate it. This is precisely how we come to the hundreds of decisions we make on a daily basis, for our conscious thought allows us to know the steps we should take based on what we currently think. Conversely, when we have our conscious mind set upon a certain perspective or decision, it becomes practically impossible for an opposing idea to dictate your direction. Pride, arrogance, and any other negative perspective can significantly impede our truer course if we allow these thoughts to prevent our deeper understanding.

The subconscious mind is vastly different, and in many ways is a mystery to our conscious being. There has been significant debate on the subject of the subconscious reality, especially as to whether or not it exists as a fundamental aspect of our thinking. There is little doubt, however, that there is a unique aspect of our thinking that goes beyond the conscious realm. Indeed, each of us has experienced the phenomenon that comes from interacting from our subconscious thought.

Nelson Mandela, for example, knew deep down in his being that freedom and change would occur at some point in his life. His most inspiring assurance came from a poem written by a now-unknown author. The defining quote from the poem inspired him to maintain his original thought form: "I am the captain of my soul; the master of my fate."

This one sentence holds the key to all of our thought existence. The captain in this example is the active thought that allows you to consciously know your current reality. Controlling your thoughts is essential to maintaining a balance that will lead to future thought and ultimate change. Had Mr. Mandela allowed his thought to sway from his firm belief in his just cause or eventual freedom, his thoughts clearly would have taken a significantly different turn at some point in the 25 years he was confined. Being the captain of your thought is essential to surviving the complexities of a thought form and the reality base of that thought.

Conversely, the soul is comparable to the idea that your subconscious thought is as wide and far-reaching as the sea itself, and the various obstacles and illusions come from the depths of this thought. Arguably, your subconscious thought is far more superior and in a perfect state at all times, yet it is wholly dependent on the conscious interpretation of any and all thoughts. The idea of the iceberg is the best universally descriptive image of conscious vs. subconscious thought. Though the tip of the berg seems mountainous in our physical representation and understanding, the remaining 90% of it is underneath the water, and this remaining percentage is the actual strength it its movement in relation to the water source. Nevertheless, the iceberg itself is only possible and existent because it is part of the entire water source in general. What we know consciously is but a small fraction of what we know subconsciously. And what we know subconsciously is only available to our Soul and

Mind based on our relation with the Universal Intelligence, i.e. the water source.

Subconscious thought is also a part of your thinking that is free from all the external realities that your conscious thought deals with on a daily basis. Opposite our conscious thought, which is influenced and impacted by every aspect of the outside world and determined by all of our human senses, the subconscious realm is only influenced by our conscious direction: hence the phrase "captain of my soul." Since your subconscious thought is superior, yet defined by the inferior conscious mind, there is a level of trust that must be adhered to by your conscious thought. This adherence necessarily allows one to know the subconscious direction will inevitably determine the reality you choose, all based on your original thought form.

The universal and individual experiences of déjà vu, coincidences, thinking of a person and then seeing them shortly after, having a dream that came true, an inspirational idea coming from seemingly out of nowhere, a voice speaking to you when no one was around – all of these examples are experiences that we have all had, yet most often, we have passed them off as insignificant or, even worse, as illusions with no basis to our lives. In reality, these are most significant experiences, and should never be overlooked. They are the bridge being formed between your conscious thought and the element of the subconscious thought. The more we listen to these guiding elements of our thought process, the clearer our original thought form becomes.

The idea that your subconscious mind is vastly superior to your conscious mind is a very difficult concept to understand, let alone apply, to your daily life. But if you truly want to find meaningful and lasting change, you must believe with all your being that this is true. There are many experiences that you have had where you could never fully determine how you develop the thought process that became your reality. Deciding on a career, meeting the love of your life, determining where to live – all are based on a conscious reality-centered thought and a single thought form. It is our subconscious thought that brought about the complexities of the thought sequence, and the thought sequence that established the progressive steps to the original thought becoming the reality-based result.

Change

Do you want to change your life? If you are like me, you ask yourself this question constantly and throughout various moments of your life. But as frequently as we may question our own motivations, most of us hardly give the actuality of change a second thought. In such a way, it may seem that considerations often become nothing more fleeting ideas that travel innocently throughout your mind. However, these fleeting and reoccurring ideas are not quite so ephemeral; they maintain a constant emotional drive within you. Like many of your most important thoughts, they exist throughout every part of you. When you do actively think about the origin of these ideas, you may truly start to take control of them. Though it is undeniably a difficult thing to change your life in such an engaged manner, it may also be the easiest thing in the world; the answers already exist in you.

The truth is, your life (and all life) changes in the blink of an eye. Positively or negatively, there is always a moment when one's life pivots in a different direction, or an event becomes a necessary catalyst. Oftentimes, you never see the change approach, although for all intents and purposes you are looking in the right direction and prepared for alteration. At other times, change appears to come from out of nowhere, and is therefore totally unexpected. But whether change is construed as positive or negative, no one can deny its inevitability. Change simply *happens,* and so it is that every single person on Earth deals with change constantly throughout their life. Consequently, the ability for you to control change is based completely on your attention to what you want to change.

Paying attention to what you want and making decisions to reach your goal is so important that it defines the level of consistency in your life. Everything that you are, everything that you possess, everything you have become, is based on the single idea that you have chosen it to be so. While it may at first seem disagreeable to accept that you have selected the negative situations that have occurred in your life, doing so means that you fully understand the extent of your control. You are in control of your life, and therefore in control of your fate and your destiny. You control your future when you start to control your present, based on learning from (not reliving) your past

"I am the captain of my soul, the master of my destiny"

When you begin to understand that your thoughts and actions are wholly dependent on your emotional impressions, you will realize that you are indeed the conductor of your life. Although many people believe that their lives are based on chance and luck, this is in fact a misconception which could not be further from truth. Considering the idea that you are the captain of your soul, you will recognize that your essence, the part of you that never changes, is your soul. Your soul is separate from your mind and body. Your soul is your unwavering connection to Life, and it is the best part of you. Ironically, the soul is the one part of life that many of us tend to most ignore or overlook.

Taking charge of your soul is the only way you will be able to take charge of your life. The soul is the entirety of your emotional strength and intelligence, and while the general consensus within society is that emotions are the most fragile (and therefore the most unreliable) part of human existence, this too is a false concept that we have been led and even taught to believe from a very young age.

In truth, individual emotions are paramount, more crucial above every other aspect of yourself, and so must be thoroughly understood if you wish to have any lasting personal development or success. As a collective society, individual emotions are less paramount and often contradictory to societal development profiting from the mass opinion, which is perhaps why there is currently such a wide-reaching divide splitting the world's societies. Still, what a collective society wants and becomes is so drastically different than what the individual needs that a fight for individual freedom is becoming more and more prevalent.

We are unique and individual, all 6.5 billion of us on the planet, yet there is one aspect that connects us all together: the Soul. Emotions are the only part of life we all share in exactly the same way. The feeling of Love is no different in you than it is in any other person. In all of us, love feels the same. Likewise, fear, happiness, and truth – each elicits the same sensation in every unique individual, to the effect that your emotions feel the same for you as they do for the complete stranger sitting next to you. When you begin to understand that your emotions are what connect you to the greater essence of Life, then you can start to understand the significance of the fact that your emotions comprise the force that produces your life's change.

How do you feel right now? What makes you happy or sad? What makes you smile throughout the day, and how do you feel about YOU? If you want to understand how emotions play the most important part of your life, you need to know how you feel right now, and in virtually every moment of your life. How do your emotions change based on the context of your day? When you go to work, how do you feel? If you are unemployed, how do you feel? When you interact with your parents, wife or friends, how do you feel? How do YOU feel? It is imperative that you know your emotions at every instance of your life, for it is with this knowledge that you will start to understand the incipient direction your life will take. Since your future is based on present moments connected together, it is enormously important that you always know how you feel – not in retrospect, but in the moment: right now.

Your emotions are the vehicle in which your thoughts travel, while the physical world is a representation of what your thoughts construct. Therefore, if you are having a bad day or week, you are certainly feeling "bad," which means you are mentally centered or preoccupied with "bad" thoughts. This preoccupation inevitably leads to "bad" actions (whether you realize it or not and whether or not you intend to generate "bad" consequences). It is not as if you are purposefully trying to think connotatively destructive thoughts, but since your feelings are the basis for what you think, and your thoughts determine the actions you take, then it stands to reason that your actions follow your thoughts which stem from your feelings in a consistently cyclical process.

Only when you begin to recognize the consistent cyclical relationship between your Soul, Mind and Body, are you then able to bring balance to them and yourself. It is not unusual to have difficult emotional moments, but it is within your power to understand and restore equilibrium. It is true that life is more fun when you're happy, but it is hardly realistic or even possible to have a life of constant and uncontested happiness. Typically, the human cycle of emotions is more volatile, as the different experiences you have throughout your day are a matter of moment to moment change.

Emotions are nevertheless a part of individual spectrums, and together they make up the sum of your emotional life. Love and hate, happy and sad, strong and weak – they all fall on their respective spectrums, and like the controls of a radio's output (i.e., volume, base and tremble) the basis of your life depends on how you handle the controls of your feelings which are, day to day and based off of your personal experiences, constantly needing adjustment. Throughout any given day, truth is the most important emotion within your life. Thus, it is imperative that you always practice truth spiritually, intellectually and physically.

There is no room in your life for false feelings, thoughts, or actions. Do not walk through your life feeling, thinking, and doing false things, for this will ultimately be the resistance to anything good you desire for your life. If you ever wonder why things don't seem to change for the better, take a good look at how truthful you are with yourself and those you interact with. You may realize that in fact, *you* are the very resistance that is preventing your personal progress and ultimate success from happening.

When you contemplate the change you want, you have to know the truth behind what you want to change. Are you unhappy, and seeking happiness? Then the only logical first step to take is to identify what it is that currently makes you unhappy. But often when asked the question "What makes you unhappy?" a person's natural first response is an unassuming: "I don't know," just like when were asked to answer a question in grade school. The truth is: you truly do know. Describing the intimate depths of this knowledge to another person is not necessarily relevant; it isn't absolutely vital that someone else know why you are unhappy. It is only important for you to know. Though consideration of feelings can be painful, self-denial or ignorance toward your feelings only leads to the suppression of growth and prevention of emotional balance. Without the understanding of feelings to positively develop your emotional balance, your feelings will always seem shrouded or inconsistent, for you will be less in control of your emotional state.

If you journey through your day knowing why you experience certain emotions based on specific circumstances, you will begin to make the positive changes that you want for your life. Whatever it is you feel at a given moment, there is a spectrum of that feeling that can turn in any direction you desire. You simply have to decide how best to direct your emotional fluctuations, and then you may practice control over your feelings. For example, if you feel anger over a spouse's behavior, it is naturally very easy to remain focused on that anger or frustration. Generally this concentration snowballs, develops into an argument, and leads to even deeper and more damaging frustration. But assuming that there are not significant underlying issues, if you recognize the cyclical relationship on the spectrum of patience and anger, you will find that peace is typically restored the moment you focus on the feeling of patience. Like all other feelings, you will find that patience is completely within your control. Our tendency toward anger is a destructive one, as anger, like oxygen to a fire, continues to feed the negative emotions.

Often, the frustration and anger you feel at certain moments is nothing more than a natural feeling. It is practically impossible to go through your day with uncontested happiness, but it is just as unusual to feel deep-seated anger or frustration for long periods of time. If you are constantly feeling a sense of discontent by way of any negative emotion, there is an emotional issue that has not been resolved. When you confront the negative emotions that arise throughout your life and really contemplate their origin, you will find a better perspective to help change that constant, draining feeling.

Whatever "bad" events have happened in your life and however hurt you felt as result, you will only ever feel the good in your life when you let the negative feelings go. Stop holding on to them. Stop allowing them to dictate your life, and then you will see the ease with which the good enters your life and expands to fill the place left by the bad. Truth, Love, and Patience become so much easier to feel when you are not creating walls of negativity structured by the schematics of past experiences.

We all want to love, to feel truth, to be patient, yet that you are only able to begin feeling by letting go of any resistance that holds you back; the negative emotions that came from past negative experiences are nothing more than a part of a memory that has been molded, binding you to feel a particular, unpleasant way. But it is just as easy for you to let the negative emotions subside and in doing so you will eventually find the happiness you seek.

"Imagine the change you feel, and your actions will always follow the lead"

Make no mistake it is very difficult to be in a situation where your emotion is prevalent for too long. Nevertheless, it is relatively impossible to be consistently on either end of an emotional spectrum. In fact, emotions are like waves: the form always flows back to its original state. If you think of your feelings in this way, it is clear that there are moments when you are extremely happy, terribly sad, enthusiastically excited, but it is also clear that those feelings subside and allow your return to a consistent, level emotional state.

It is this stable emotional base, the feeling that you carry within you throughout your day, that causes your identifiable personality to become a reflection of your most consistent emotions. The level of fluctuation between emotional states is the defining characteristic of your emotional balance, and the truest reflection of your personality. There are biological explanations and exceptions, of course, for the most extreme cases of emotion (such as depression for a pervasive and constant sadness), but for our purposes, we are discussing a holistic response to the natural self rather than delving into the idea of diagnosis disorders. This is not to say that such maladies do not exist, but rather that the diagnoses are frequently overused and often issued in grave error.

Determining the state of your emotional balance is essential, as doing so will lead you to discovering the connection between your feelings and your thoughts (and subsequently, your actions). If you are in a happy state, your thoughts will inevitably follow this state of being. Likewise, if you are sad, your perspective will follow the lead and see things from that point of view. Obviously, the ideas your thoughts navigate lead to the actions you physically take.

"Change is a feeling that produces thought, thought is a perception that forces action,   action is a decision that balances feeling"

When you are truly centered with what you want in some aspect of your life with little urge for change and you sense in your life a welcome balance, you are on the path of least resistance. And while there are many different aspects of your life that you may find need changing, it is best to begin your journey with the most important change. Simply know what makes you the most happy, and you will find your starting point for developing a better, stronger self.

Personally, my happiest moment developed following the unhappiest moment of my life; I found myself homeless after more than a decade of working as an effective family counselor. Now, considering that I helped many families deal with the very issue from which I suffered, it seems unbelievable to me that I could have ended up in such a seemingly terrible situation. But I also now know just how emotionally unbalanced my life had become: the changes I wanted for myself were not reflected in my life. I came to realize that there was no way for me to "fix" my life unless it toppled over completely, and I was forced to start anew.

I have always said that finding my life in utter turmoil was the best worst thing that ever happened to me. I certainly wouldn't wish the loneliness and isolation on anyone, and I now know what it feels like to be empty of Love and Patience. But I know, too, especially after climbing up to such professional heights from such a lowly upbringing only to be torn back down, that change can be real when you want it to be. And the opposite is also true; if you do not truly know what you want for your life or how to change the things you truly want for you, the life you build is in serious jeopardy of crumbling around you. This is often why we tend to feel as if our life is falling apart at certain moments – we are internally struggling with false representations of our physical world as it often serves to contradict our internal feelings and beliefs.

Be Aware of what you expect or Beware of what you get

Life's greatest gift is our ability to make positive change in our lives. You are capable of attaining the life that you truly want and capable of building a better more successful you. There is positive value in recognizing the specific parts of your life that you feel need to be changed, and so you must often think about those seemingly negative facets of your existence. Never shy away from the feelings that are most impressed on you, for whether those feelings are good or bad, it is only by confrontation will you find the need to change them.

One must not wait for the right moment to change...start now!

Change starts with emotional strength. When you feel there is something you want to change, you have to then begin considering what that change would be and what forms it could possibly take. The feeling of change is a process. Your life will typically follow a course of thought and action. It is hardly possible to change the physical reality of your anticipated change immediately, but then again, the physical reality of your change actually does start the moment you feel and then think of the change you want. Knowing what you want to change is so much more important than knowing precisely the manner in which you will create the change.

Most aspects of a person's life cannot change immediately. But that is only true if you expect to reach the end result of the intended change immediately. Change itself does not develop instantaneously, and most of the time, one will likely never find that instant gratification results from immediate change. Change is the accumulation of the moments you decide to change, as a process. For instance, if your change was to lose 25 pounds, then it is impossible that such an alteration could occur in a single day; however, the process does, in fact, start today. Take a 2-mile walk today, and then eat healthy at every meal today. In time, in the pursuit of a process, you will be guaranteed the results you desire. Change happens at the moment you commit to it, and you will come to understand that the weight you wish to lose was lost as a product of the choice you made.

The level of change you want for your life is inconsequential. The process is the same for each idea that is unique to you. Weight, health, relationships, work, money – the process is the same for everything. However, it is hardly possible to bring change to many different issues at a given time. It is better to choose the most important change you feel for you right now, and to focus on that vision completely. You will find that once you deal with your most important change, the other changes you wish to make to your life have either followed suit with your renewed intentions, or have become easier to navigate. You will have gained valuable experience of the process of change by feeling your change and thinking about why you want to change, which inevitably leads to the action required to bring about the change you want. And be assured, you will never be able to predict the moment change occurs. As a participant in a process, your only focus should be to know what you want to change and why you want to change it. The magic moments in life will deliver the how and the when for you.

Magic Moments

We have all experienced special moments in our lives when the details of what we want seem to come together like minor miracles. Or perhaps something you needed so desperately had become a reality, even though it seemed so unbelievable that it happened or could have happened. These are not miracles by any sense. These are not moments where your God neither reaches down and orchestrates a miracle, nor directs his angels to give you that which you want most. These are magic moments that happen as frequently as you think about your dreams. You create magic moments when you establish a consistency in knowing what thing you want, and why it is that you want it.

Meeting the person you eventually married or with whom you had a longstanding relationship is maybe the most common form of a magic moment. And what about moments where you were hired for a new job, were promoted seemingly unexpectedly, or found your ideal new home? The truth is, these moments are not unexpected at all. In fact, they only occurred because you were not expecting them; you felt and thought of them consistently, setting them as goals. And dreaming of these moments, feeling and thinking of them consistently, is the only way that these magic moments became your reality. You were absolutely thinking of the person you wanted to be with, just as surely as you were thinking of the details of a new job or place to live. If you look back at the major moments of your life, you will see just how plentiful magic moments were, precisely because you felt a need to have them and thought strongly about why you wanted them.

Your life is not based on chance. This is perhaps the biggest theoretical obstacle most of us struggle with when it comes to understanding personal development. There is no such thing as chance or luck. If you think about the very existence of our universe, at least that which we can comprehend from our subjective experience, it is clear that there is a special synchronicity within everything that occurs. There is an intelligent force creating and controlling everything. Dark matter and energy, the theoretical glue that holds the magnificent substance within the universe together, makes up 4/5ths of our entire existence, yet we can neither touch nor describe it, anymore than we can touch or describe light.

However, there actually "is" an intelligent force that makes up the entire universe, and you are part of this very special reality. Millions and millions of stars are born everyday out of massive gaseous clouds deep in the space of each galaxy, clouds that are millions and millions of light years long. Not to mention the billions of galaxies that exist and we know that these billions of galaxies are only what we can see with our most advanced observation machines. The Universe is constantly moving. The Universe is constantly growing adding more and more substance, all while maintaining complete order in every moment.

It is practically impossible to determine an end to the Universe, because even though it is amazing to consider billions of galaxies, it's clear that the universe certainly doesn't end there. Even if it did, what would be at the end of the physical universe? Nothing? Even nothing is part of the something. And for every amazing scientific mind suggesting there is an end to the universe, there is another equally gifted intellectual that refutes these claims.

And the truth will always remain; we will never know the true extent of the universe any more than we could travel to even the next galaxy. But our level of understanding is indeed perfectly synchronized in every way right down to the smallest detail, for we know that we are indeed part of a magical universal force filled with movement that resembles chaos. Yes, the universe is perfect, and you are part of this very special phenomenon. That means that you are nothing less than perfect. Yet one of the most universally accepted thoughts is that no one is perfect, which is as wrong as the former belief that our Earth was flat.

Everything we know about our universe beyond the most advanced machines is a guess, and while there are many educated guesses, they are established based on limits we have created, the same ideas that we have been taught our entire life: "All good things end" or "If something is too good to be true, it likely is" or more specifically, "Everything must come to an end." These ideas are simply not true. If something is too good to be true, it is because you don't believe completely in the good things that you want, and if a good thing ends, it is because it becomes something better or different. And if it is too good to be true, then it may just be bad, but that is because you created that idea from a feeling of reservation or negative energy.

Considering hindsight is an excellent reflective exercise, examine your past for the sole purpose of discovering a pattern. Once you begin to reflect upon it, you will realize that every single time that a profound event occurred in your life, it was you who created such a magic moment. There is a magic to Life itself, and whichever spiritual ideas or religious order you believe in, it is your belief in something that creates everything you want. As long as you recognize the power you hold in developing your dreams, your developments may be limitless. However, the opposite of your dreams coming true is just as possible if you express the sort of feelings that tend to work against your intended purpose.

Every moment of your life is a representation of your dreams. The level to which you believe in your dreams and trust that they will come true is the essential aspect of your dreams that needs the most attention. If you establish a dream, which is the same as saying you have an idea for your future, and allow self-doubt, fear, or any other negative emotion to effect the image of that dream, you are essentially creating a philosophical tug of war between what you want and why you can't have it. You may know what you want, but have counterproductively established an entire belief system on why you can't have it (ideas that you are not good enough or smart enough, that you don't deserve it or were born poor, or even that concept that dreams are just fantasies, and so on into endless other self-deprecations and assertions of doubt). Whatever your limited belief, if you think such thoughts then you are absolutely right; your dreams will not come true, and it is the same feeling and thoughts that created the dream that just as easily extinguished your wishes.

Magic moments are neither magic nor moments, they are your life in perpetual movement that is based on bringing physical reality to what you want for YOU.

If you set about thinking that magic is real and that out of nothing something is produced, then this concept will likely delude you and prevent you from ever reaching any of the good that you want for yourself. The reason you have a mediocre life, or always seem to get so close to that which you want only to be thwarted at the last minute, is because you allow passivity to dominate your direction rather than taking active control of your life in every way. You will be successful if you imagine this to be true and stick to this image.

Oftentimes, we allow our image of what we want (even though we know so clearly why we want it) to be controlled by that other part of us that seems to push against our ambitions and goals. We may even infect our feelings with ideas that we know are simply not true, and thereby negatively realigns our emotions. The truth is, if you can think an idea, and know why you want it, then there is absolutely nothing that could possibly stand in your way. Nothing can keep you from that achievement you desire, except for yourself.

Herein lies the crucial point of personal success. When you have doubt, this is a natural reflection. Can I be a great teacher? Am I capable of being a loving parent? Am I smart enough for the position I want? These are all important questions to ask yourself when you're contemplating or have been confronted with a new change to your life, or even the possibility of change. To ask the question is an important component, as it allows you to prepare and strengthen your thoughts and skills to better adapt for the thing that you want. But it should never derail your feelings and thoughts in any respect. Self-doubt adds no value to personal development, and will only create resistance if left to develop within the process of change.

Reflecting this point is a scientific study conducted with a Russian long distance running team. When scientists had asked one group of athletes to think about their run before practicing and another group to simply exercise and then run, the group that thought then practiced did significantly better during their run than the group that jumped right into practice. The implications of this study and others like it suggest the strong correlation between thought and successful results.

So-called magic moments are not a chance encounter based on a flimsy idea of which direction your life is headed. Another key example occurs in consideration of any entrepreneur or successful businessperson. You may have heard a universal description that the secret to achieving success is 90% inspiration and 10% perspiration, with an element of luck arising vaguely somewhere during the process.

This commonly accepted idea of what it takes to be successful in business describes exactly the idea of creating magic moments. Feeling the desire to be in business and then taking the majority of your time thinking through your thoughts of the right product, service and ultimate direction of the business is vital.

Once your thought process reaches a point where the urge for action is pushing you to make a start, the relative ease of following your thought process seems simple and almost as though you had already taken action. The business unfolds like a story already written. That is, apart from a single exception: it is your story, and you have already written it based in your thought process. While there are adjustments and adaptations that will always come up in the physical reality of making your dreams come true, there are not so many changes that it will strays from the core of your image. It is the goal, outcome, or destination that it is most important to adhere to, and having the flexibility and wherewithal to stay focused on maintaining the image of what you're working towards that matters.

That element of luck therefore, has nothing to do with an invisible force that inexplicably brings good fortune to a person or rains down on the select few who are blessed by the mysterious intelligence of the universe. No, it is instead the undervalued ability to feel your way through life, and then allowing your thoughts to follow the lead of your emotional intelligence to get that which you want. Then the goal is to take action, while always, in each moment, allowing your feelings to remain centered. With this process, you are able to guide your success, from the invisible to the contemplative and eventually to an action sequence. By allowing Life to establish the positioning points to develop your thoughts into reality, you are creating your own luck.

We have all felt the urge to take action, and we can all often think back to significant moments when we could practically plan out how perfect things would fall into place if we could only get something. You could, for example, start a new business if you could borrow the start-up money, and pay the loan back with the profit you turn in less than a month. Or, once you get accepted to college, you could get a great career, and quickly pay off the student loans you took out. It is essential to envision the idea, but to become too abstract in your thoughts only allows you to forget the importance of actually knowing what you want. It is almost blinding to only focus on the end result, that of reaching your goal. In reality, the process of reaching the goal is just as important as the goal itself.

If, for instance, you suddenly have an idea for a great business and believe that you just need the start-up money, then you might be failing to see the actual process. You have jumped from an abstract idea to starting the business in relatively no time at all. One important criterion is missing in the process, the ability to reflect and foresee potential problems, and creative adaptations that may allow a goal to become reality based on your thoughts. There are many times when the original idea is adjusted, shifted, and manipulated in your thoughts well before the action is initiated; doing so will means you will avoid the most ill-conceived of processes.

Thought processes exist to understand the limitations, potential pitfalls, and even the realistic expectations. Critiquing your own idea or ambition is so important, as it allows you to truly see the effect of the idea or ambition, and will help guide you through the intellectual process of making that idea a reality (while also preventing you from following a course that is not suited for you in particular). By basing your decisions on a realistic aspect of you, the talents, skills and resources you have today will forge your path for tomorrow. But jumping the points in the process will surely prevent the magic from happening.

Also, your dreams and aspirations are yours alone. Asking another person if your dreams are right is just as ineffective as allowing your thoughts to jump from point A to Z without considering the necessary points in between. The reality of your dreams must always be grounded in the factuality of your feelings. It is hardly likely that your parents or closest confidant are able to understand how you feel about certain thoughts. In some cases, those you consult will try to inadvertently guide you based on what they think about the idea, with little consideration for how you feel about the idea.

For example, if you suddenly develop a strong urge to be a doctor, yet you only have a G.E.D., it is extremely unlikely you would be ready for medical school before you start to prove your academic commitment. While no one closest to you can determine whether you are capable of being a successful doctor, nor should they ever suggest such an opinion, they should express the necessary concerns you might need to consider in achieving such a lofty goal: such an academic endeavor will be difficult, you have to do better in school, you need a strong commitment, and so forth. Such concerns support your ideas and allow you to confirm what you should be already thinking.

Whatever your ambition is, your achievement rests completely on your ability to be honest with your feelings. If you truly want a thing and sincerely think through the process of how you may get it, there is nothing that will prevent you from reaching your goal. Such consideration means that you will reach your goal, for you will have dealt with the biggest obstacle in your way: yourself.

Magic moments are a necessary part of your internal life becoming a reality. They are directly connected to the part of your dreams that ultimately forces the imaginary into a reality. Your thought is much like the seed of a tree. Once it is ready to drop to the ground, the seed mysteriously makes its way under the earth, where it may open. Then it becomes roots that reach for steady, secure ground. And when it is ready, there comes a moment when the growth must pierce the ground and open to the world above. Your thoughts work in precisely this way. You have to plant the seed of feeling, the right idea, and then you must patiently wait for the moment, the magic moment, that pierces from the imaginary to become a physical reality. Rest assured, this moment always comes with whatever you dream. Good or bad, the reality will always make its way from the seat of your soul, so it is extremely important to make absolutely sure your feelings are centered, and that you are therefore creating the right thoughts for your life.

Simply to create the idea based on your feelings is not enough. There is more to the creative process than simply developing ideas to better your future. So far, we have only discussed the process of ideas becoming reality. You must also begin to shape you feelings by understanding what is of most value in your life. These are ideals that are the same for everyone, and just as emotions feel the same for each individual throughout the world, the guiding principles for your life are also the same for you as they are for every person. The more you understand the process of finding your guiding light, the easier it is to always find the positive direction in your life.

Your soul is your guiding light. Truth, Love, and Patience are the trilateral points to which you become aware of your connection to the universe. Truth, Love, and Patience are at the core of everything ever created in the universe, and since man is the only species of its kind developed with the ability to feel, thin, and act, it is clear that we must feel, think, and act with the ideals that are ingrained in every aspect of the universe: the need to understand Truth, Love, and Patience.

The entirety of human existence is based on the trilateral connection caused by one's understanding of their Soul, Mind and Body. In order to be a complete person, you must understand each of these aspects of your personal development. When the internal thought is ready to pierce the surface, you must be prepared to see the imagined ambition successfully achieved. The magic moment is indeed significant to piercing the surface, but your physical adaptability completely determines the level of success you eventually achieve. All too often, people finally see their dream established in reality only to become complacent, assuming their efforts have been rewarded – yet the magic moment is only the boost in the process. Your continuous actions effect the ultimate achievement. Now that your feeling has produced the thought and the magic moment has occurred, it is your physical ability that determines your future success.

The Soul, Mind and Body are the three components of everything that is mystical and magical in human life, and the ability to tap into the greatness of each component defines and structures your greatness. To have a mind full of thoughts and purpose without truth and love to guide your direction will produce unbalance and inconsistency in your life. When you strengthen your soul, your mind will become your magnificent strength, and you will be led to a fulfilled life from which your action and persistence will surely prosper.

Magic moments are real, and they occur frequently throughout your life, especially when you truly want the moment to happen. A magic moment is the mysterious way the universe presents the dream, the how and when the thing happens. Understand your Soul, strengthen your Mind, and control your Body, and magic moments will always represent the best of you and give you everything that you desire in this world.

Patience

Man spends so much time pondering the single most important question of all existence: does God exist? And if so, where? Every thought you have regarding your life and ultimate destination is based on this question, and man either spends countless hours trying to crack the riddle, or wasteful hours in an effort to avoid the reality of the answer. But the answer is already within you. We are reminded often by a feeling of deep-seated completeness, a sensation of wholeness to all of everything. Yet we allow the feeling to pass by without giving it real consideration.

When man feels the patience within, the truth becomes easier to sense, and the answers he seeks become clearer to his mind. Whether you search for the answer to a simple problem or that of a complex issue, the process to the answer is the same: Patience. Man can think he practices patience, but the very idea of patience, as with truth, is in actuality quite subtle and difficult to grasp. There is no expiration date for patience; it cannot be handled from man's mind. It requires feeling. The ever present balance between giving up and moving forward is based primarily on the subtleties of patience.

How many times have you pounded your fist on your steering wheel, or slammed your hand on a table in anger for not getting your way, or when something perceivably goes wrong for you? When you have your heart set on something or try to make things work a certain way, it is frustrating when things just don't seem to work out. Think, for example, about the times when you start the day in a "bad" way only to have it get worse throughout. It's ridiculous how perfect that seems to work out sometimes, but if you changed your perspective in the moment when you felt your day was going to be bad, this would help you change the course of the day; it will likely allow the opposite to become true. These are the magic moments that are deeply connected to the patience one feels. Impatience breeds negativity, while patience promotes a deeper sense of stability and consistency in your life.

If you feel that the day is starting out "bad", then doesn't that theoretically suggest that the day is going to continue that way? Why does a moment of one or two seemingly isolated incidents morph into an entire days' worth of "bad" incidents, and ultimately become a "bad" day? In reality, it is the thought that you follow in your mind that determines the course of action your day takes. And if you are only considering today, then it is safe to argue that tomorrow leads from today, and should in all likelihood resemble similar experiences of "goodness" or "badness."

This is precisely why many people find themselves with weeks and weeks of "bad" experiences, or begin to suggest that nothing ever goes their way, or that things always seem to get worse for them. This may be true for a single day, but if you ever verbally or mindfully said these things then, yes: you are right; you are having a bad day which will turn into a bad week, month, year, life, etc. The feeling perpetuates the reality, and you must have balance between the two in order to experience positive growth.

The balance of your reality is based on your mind's level of understanding of your feelings, coupled with the reality of an experience. When you try to control the outcome of your experiences in the physical world, you become both the decider and controller of your destiny. However, the idea that man controls his physical world from only the conscious thought is the reason most people stumble and fall throughout their life.

There is only one way to shape a person's life: through feeling and possessing the patience to understand the deeper essence and strength of emotional intelligence. Your feeling shapes your Soul, your thought shapes your reality, and your physical experiences can never be developed any other way. Before a carpenter begins constructing a house, he feels the urge to build it, and then he thinks about the house first. Before an athlete competes, she feels the desire to train and thinks of training first. Before a person does anything in the physical word, feeling and then thought always precedes the action.

If you had practiced the true nature of patience in every moment, your life would have taken many different twists and turns. Of course, you would still have had bad experiences, but with the bad come the good, as with winter comes spring. We live our lives with a storm always approaching or fleeing, depending on our perspective. If you have the ability to understand this, then you are that much closer to finding the patience to carry you through even the toughest moments you have yet to encounter.

This is not a discussion of judgment. We are only narrowing down the concept of what is learned in the physical world, and how that knowledge may shape your eternal life. We are all here on Earth for a fraction of a second in comparison to the infinite vastness and timelessness of the invisible world. Some people become so clear about the invisible world in the physical reality that we call them saints and wise men, prophets or seers; but in truth, these are the people who were able to find solitude in their ability to feel truth and love, and who also have the patience to allow truth and love to solidify over the course of their time on Earth.

But the most humble of all wise ones, namely Jesus and Buddha, have always said any other human can find in clarity what they have found. It is not a secret to know the depths of your soul, to find truth, or to become closer to the Universal Intelligence; it is a natural right, just as the redwood seed will always become a giant natural beauty with the right nourishment from Life, along with the inherent servitude to grow. Man, too, is born with an inherent purity that will allow him to grow into greatness, but he must also take the nourishments of Life while cleansing his soul of anything that will detract from his growth.

The patience to wait for the rightness to come to you is as natural as the shifting of the winds. Your life is a natural organism that is connected to the greater organism of all life. We control our conscious destiny, but the road to our greatness is paved by another source altogether, Life. When you want for something, such as a new occupation or a healthy relationship, it is your responsibility to feel what you want and then think through what you want and truly know why you want such a change. Just as we must first think before anything is manifested to us in reality, our thoughts are always more powerful than our actions. But it is our feelings that act as the driving force.

If man can choose the right options for him while being completely clear about why he desires those specific things, his life will be as if nature was blooming the prettiest of flowers. Just as a tulip can never grow to be a rose bush, nor a dandelion into a carnation, our lives are created for the sole intention of reaching our personal greatness.

There are more than 6 Billion people in the world, and each one is no more alike than the next. We are each individual and original, and have amazingly different life experiences. Yet we continue to share in common the most every emotional elements of life.

Though we are born into the world of the I and make distinct paths for ourselves, we often forget that without other people in society, Life would be a vast realm of nothingness. We need those around us, because within the collective element is the source of all knowledge. The defining quality of life is to understand the true source of your personal greatness, and then to share your knowledge with those around you.

But even this does not secure a person's tenure of finding greatness. Even the best of men have fallen from great heights – history is riddled with many examples of a person reaching an ultimate destination, only to have their world come crashing down around them. It certainly doesn't matter from whence you came if the destination you reach is on ill terms within your Soul. Wanting the good things life has to offer, whatever those are to you, (a loving wife, beautiful children, a nice home, a great job) are natural desires in the physical world. At least if you adhere to the beliefs of a society that promotes these ideas, then these natural desires must be sought.

But the problem is that when you want for the sake of wanting (because that is what seems to be the general consensus for "want") then you are limiting the course of what you receive. If you set out to achieve your want with only a half-hearted idea that you will actually get everything you want, then this also limits what you are able to receive.

In general, people do not believe that what the mind conceives is achieved. In truth, everything your mind conceives is absolutely achieved, as long as you allow truth and love to be your guides, and practice to see your exact dreams reach fruition. The closer you adhere to your ideal creation within your Soul and Mind, the more accurate the physical representation becomes. Life is not based on chance; it is based on the law that what you think about you attract to you, or as we find it phrased in the more popular terminology: the law of attraction.

If a woman wants to be a teacher and has wanted such her entire life, then it would be wise for her to commit to that thought within her mind. She should consider herself a teacher in her mind, and then take all the steps necessary to fulfill that goal. If she truly wants to be a teacher, and instead decides for a host of reasons that her life is more suited as a hair dresser, then she is clearly wronging herself and ultimately causing more pain than just the idea of giving up on her dream.

If you think through the person you want to be and then honestly decide the right framework for the person you want to be, your next step should always be to commit to that image. You must begin to truly know that you will make that concept within your mind a reality. And to be clear, if you can think it and are agreeable to it, then there is absolutely no reason why such a desire will never transpire – unless of course, you allow doubt and concern to interfere with its manifestation along the way. But Patience is the powerful source that allows you to hold to the feeling and remain grateful that it will transpire in due time, however long it may take.

Nelson Mandela is perhaps one of the most inspiring people in modern history. He believed in the rights of his people in South Africa, and fought to end apartheid. When he was a young activist, Mandela was jailed for his opposition to the South African government. As a result, he spent more than 25 years in prison for speaking up in the name of Truth and Love. In all those years that he was held captive, the most important strength he had was the ability to be Patient and allow this to strengthen his Soul. Indeed, a few years after being released from prison, Nelson Mandela had become the first black president of South Africa. He believed in what he felt, allowed this feeling to guide his thought, and practiced patience to see it revealed.

The ideas that you create in your mind are better than the physical reality, and while there are certain actions that man is required to perform to bridge the connection from the thought world to the physical reality, there is no quality more important than patience. Having the patience to know that Life will allow magical things to fall into place without you being able to see the when and how they happen, such are the magic moments in our life that many of us overlook. Yet examples are transparent in every way and everywhere. Life is precious in that way: amazing things are created for one's life, and all you must do is let go of the control and simply focus on the clarity of your ideas.

The clearest example of a magic moment is when two people meet and their lives are soon conjoined. It is no secret that a single being on Earth is destined to be united with another, but the solidity of that adjournment is wholly dependent on their ability to know who they want for a partner. It is hardly plausible that one might choose anyone on the planet that they want, precisely because there are two people, not one individual, who play a part in the process of unification. What is the truth in regards to meeting your partner? To be sure, you have always had an idea of what your partner would be like; every precise detail has been part of you since you held the thought. And when you meet that person – this is where the notion of love at first sight was developed. Your feeling has already sensed the person you wanted to be with.

The reason most relationships fail is not because love is not present nor commitment affirmed. The chains of commitment keep relationships together; the power of passion is the only force strong enough to shatter those chains. Patience is the key motivator to finding the "love" we all search for on earth. The more you believe in and wait for the perfect image of the person you want to share your life with, the more success you will have in being happier sooner with your ideal mate.

You can never predict when that special moment will happen. Browsing for a book at the bookstore, grocery shopping, bumping into someone in the elevator, walking around the corner in a remote out-of-the-way place – there are as many moments of magic as one could possibly imagine, and the secret to real magic, of course, is that man does not and cannot control what the invisible knows. That is the true nature of patience. You have no control over how and when a thing happens. You cannot predict when the love of your life will enter your life, nor can you predict how they will do so, and the more you try to control this, less likely the event will transpire.

Instead, man must learn to control the image, the idea, with absolute clarity. What do you want in a partner, what does she look like, what does he aspire to be, what does he believe, what does she love, what makes her cry, what? What? What? The details matter, and the more clearly you feel the details, the more visible the image becomes, and the more closely the real-life moment will mirror your dream.

Most people do not believe that their images produce the physical results. They believe life is based on chance and that while sometimes the things we think about come true, such matters can be passed off as coincidence. But if you look back at the most important moments of your life, you will start to see a pattern in the way Magic Moments have occurred in your existence. The moment you achieved what your mind conceived has always been magical, good magic or bad magic, because the mind does not know good from bad, it only knows what it is taught by the person's ability to provide emotional images.

Think of your connection between the mind and the physical world as you would a virtual reality. Your physical reality is an avatar, if you will. You get the options to dress, shape and provide every detail for your avatar, but only when you feel those options first. Every detail of your life is based on what you want or don't want and the stronger the impulse one way or the other, the more visible the outcome.

If you simply state to your mind that you want to be with someone without any regard for the details, then it is 100% accurate that you will meet someone, but the person will be random and less inclined to be the idea of the person you actually had in mind. Instead, you must have the patience to know that what you conceive will magically be produced in due time.

Patience is the key to all physical realities that take shape. If man practices proper patience and allows their life to grow in the process of their natural greatness, then their life will be far more bountiful than if they try to control the growth with tools beyond their understanding or ability to use. For instance, if you plant a flower, then water it as needed, trim it as required, and practice patience, that flower will grow to be a wonderful example of Life's beauty. But, if you water that flower twice as much in the hopes it will become a beautiful flower twice as fast, then you are mistaking your powers.

In your own life, you naturally have the ability to plant the seed of patience in your heart. You know what you want and why you want it, just as the gardener chooses which flower to plant in the garden. You have the ability to shape and mold what it is you want in your heart, good or bad. But it is Life's responsibility to nourish and produce the results of what you sow, and it is your responsibility to practice the patience to know the difference between what is within your control and what is not. You must learn to wait for Life to produce the results you desire.

Purpose

Purpose is the essence of who you are and the reason you live. Without even the simplest elements of purpose, you would have no drive to do anything. Every morning when you awaken, there is purpose to the start of your day. Your purpose is similar to your thought form; it begins with an original element. As Thomas Jefferson surmised, every person has the right to be the person they want to be, defined by the happiness through which they see the world.

Your life is based on the "You" that you want to be. Refining this perspective in your life is the most important element to determine the course you take. If you took a poll of every successful person throughout history, past or present, you will find a similar characteristic they all share: purpose. And most of them knew at a young age what their purpose was for their life.

Einstein knew at the young age of 5, the moment he saw the compass he received as a gift, that he was immediately drawn to the need for understanding the invisible force that controlled the needle of the compass. From that moment forward, he spent his life dedicated to finding that answer. And while he never quite found the answer he was in search of, he made such an impact that virtually imprinted his life and passion on the world forever. He is to intellectual pursuit as Buddha is to spiritual awakening, or as Jesus is to religious following.

A defining characteristic the most impassioned share is that they are people, following individual pursuits and found great success in their life. But this success was not by chance or luck, it was because they made a commitment to being the best at what they found to be their passion, their purpose. Warren Buffet, once the world's richest man, is perhaps the most amazing and successful businessman of all time. And like Einstein, he started at a young age, putting together effective home businesses as he prepared for his future success. Lemonade stands, vending machines, and amusement games – he did anything he thought that would make money, starting when he was only 10 years of age.

Unlike most successful businesspeople, Mr. Buffet built his entire empire based on thousands of individual business decisions rather than a single product or service. Unlike singular product businessmen like Bill Gates or Michael Dell, Mr. Buffet has, over the course of his life, bought and rarely sold many businesses (starting from a rundown textile factory in New England that teetered on bankruptcy). But he believed in his financial knowledge and personal ability to make sound business decisions. And he was right every single time. If you were to determine the best business-for-business professional like a pound-for-pound fighter, Buffett is considered the best in history, without equal.

We all have the ability to be successful. There is no defining limit to success. The glass ceiling is nonexistent in the realm of individual advancement. Such limitations only exist in the field of competition and personally designed limitations. And since purpose is an individual journey that is based on an independent perspective, discovering your purpose or passion is vital to knowing who you are and what your area of expertise is. And no one, not even Einstein or Buffet, is successful from the start of their journey. As anyone who ever became successful following their passion, there are many ups and downs and struggles in-between, but success is defined when you stand by your commitment to your purpose.

Athletes are unique when it comes to defining purpose. While an athletic ability hardly defines the person, however, like any profession, it is the vehicle in which one makes an impact on their world. Young children look up to famous athletes not necessarily because they have amazing moves or incredible physical abilities, but because they have a drive and passion that is easily displayed within every aspect of their play. You can practically see the purpose to which they play their game, which is simply the athlete's own drive to be the best.

Like in childhood games on the playground, winning or losing is most certainly a byproduct of playing the game. And in most every instance, winning or losing is hardly a defining point of success. Being a tennis player is perhaps the most difficult of all sports to become successful at. It is one of the only sports where the success is individual-based; each time an individual tennis player steps onto a court, they are defining their success on their own, based on their experience, which comes from their passion. Unlike baseball or basketball players, who play 100-plus games a year and have a team of 15 or 20 teammates working with them, tennis players are utterly by themselves, without even a coach to guide them, and their success on the court is based entirely on their personal drive to be their best in that moment.

The other interesting aspect of a professional athlete is that, just like Einstein and Buffet, most who have become successful at their respective sports had known they were passionate about their game from the time they could first handle the equipment. Tiger Woods, Carl Yastrzemski, and Nolan Ryan all knew at a young age what their purpose was, and they strove from that moment on to become the best in their chosen sport.

As an individual, you must know what game you are playing before you can commit to playing that game. What does your ball look like? Which sport does it belong to? Where do you go to play the game? These are abstract questions, but you must know the answer if you are going to understand the direction of your life. And while we may not have all known what our purpose was at a young age, it stands to reason you do have one. Discovering your passion is paramount to anything you do in this world.

Mother Teresa is also one of the most inspiring people throughout history. Her purpose and passion were evident, even though her chosen field was one where she voluntarily gave up her personal identity. How could a person who relinquished all of her independence and personal identity to follow the God and order she believed in so completely become a leading voice for the care and welfare of all people on Earth? It was the purpose she felt to become a supportive force within society.

Ironically, her dedication had catapulted her to international attention though her purpose was one of everyday common courtesy; she merely believed in the individual's fight for meaning. She helped thousands of people directly by providing them with a reason for living and support while they were in the process of dying. The poorest and sickest were comforted with the presence of a woman who so fully committed herself to the truest form of human civility.

By her commitment, Mother Teresa inspired millions of people to believe in a purpose that starts with the individual and spreads throughout humanity.

And unlike the most famous of athletes, Mother Teresa never expected nor welcomed personal accolades. When asked why she dedicated her life to helping others, her response was a simple one: because we all need to feel truth and love from one another, regardless of our personal stake within the world. Even the lowliest of a society, by their own choosing or otherwise, matter.

Purpose is defined by your ability to move about your world with the same sense of dedication and passion that Mother Teresa exhibited. But discovering your purpose is not measured in finding a place on the world stage. And if you set out wanting to become the most important figure in your field, you will likely not reach even a seat in your local community. Purpose is personal; it is a growing need to fill a place within the world that is right for you. It is based on your personal strengths, raw or refined, and those strengths should lend a hand to promote the greater good and add value within society. If you happen to grow substantially within while you follow your pursuit of purpose, it is likely you will become a leading proponent of that which you purposefully pursue.

Whether you are an athlete, businessperson, or spiritual advisor, the role you choose is the one that will help you find balance within your world. Your soul is connected to the greater force within the universe. Life is within you, and you are a part of something spectacular. Know that the foundations of your soul are significant to this connection, and be aware of the quiet strength you form from the moment you are born. It is your thought and purpose that allow you to express this knowledge throughout the world. It is also the part of your personal development that continues to be refined as you tap into the collective society, by following through doing your part within the world.

Having purpose is not always defined in your "job"; one could be a sanitation worker and find purpose outside of that profession. Being a great parent, volunteering your time to an important cause, providing a supportive ear to those you are closest to, all of these things or just a single one of them can be a defining purpose. There is never a closed door or filled seat when it comes to providing support and strength within your community. Everyone has a place at the table, but it is up to you to determine where you sit. If you have ever visited a counselor or psychologist, one of the subtle propositions they make without directive is allowing you to choose the seat to sit in. Not by coincidence, they have a few to choose from; one closest, one beside, or one furthest away. Which seat you choose gives the therapist a subtle reflection of how you may open up to the dialogue that will soon take place.

Imagination is the key to understanding and maintaining a keen focus on your purpose in life. Since purpose is the spark that is created from your feelings and from your soul, it is important to find the best of you in order to express the best of yourself within your community. Imagining what that best self is for you, based on the strengths and abilities you possess, is an essential piece of knowledge to have ready when you begin your journey. And often times, simply having the idea is the best first step you could take.

In order to discover your life purpose, you must first figure out what it is that you love to do. What are your hobbies? What are your interests? What are you good at doing? Do you love fashion? Do you love art? Do you love fixing things around the house? What are you passionate about? The things that we are most passionate about in life are usually part of our life's purpose. They act as the vehicles which further inspire our connection to the beauty of life.

Once you decide what you love to do, ideas for your life purpose will come to you as naturally as the water flows down a stream. Though deciding on the idea is obviously the most important first step to acting on your purpose, the natural development of the idea or career is something the Universal Intelligence controls completely. You will never know where a great idea will come from, so just follow your emotional connection to the purpose you envision, and you will come know which idea is the right one for you.

Once you have decided what purpose and passion means to you, it is important to develop a solid idea of how that is represented within your world. There is a place and position for everyone and just as individual change is a constantly occurring phenomenon with your personal development, it is the same within the collective society. There is movement and openings, adjustments and opportunities always forming and while you may not know how to begin following your passion, imagining what it will look like is the key to developing it.

I had always wanted to open up a coffee shop; a little community shop with a small number of tables and good coffee. I wanted it to be a place where people could sense the hub of the community. On the greater stage of the world it certainly wasn't a grandiose idea, but it was to be a good place, with good customers, within a community where I grew up. But for years I had thought about opening a coffee shop, and in the early stages of this thought, I had no idea where it would be, what it would look like, or even what I wanted to call it. At some point, though, I knew that I wanted to open a coffee shop.

When I stopped counseling, which I had done directly for almost 15 years and had committed to right out of college, I felt the need to stay connected to the community I worked in. But I wasn't ready to start a new career, so I did what I always thought was a good idea for me. I decided that the time was right. I found the perfect location and established Cafe West within 2 months of actively initiating the idea, even though I had passively thought about the idea for years.

My purpose in my life certainly wasn't to open up a coffee shop, nor was it a lifelong dream, an end all to my success, but it was an idea that I wanted to fulfill at some point in my life. I simply waited for the right time to take action. Life has a unique way of creating the timing and opportunities to follow through with that which we want most. Yet like meeting your future spouse, it is hardly a sequence of events that fall on your lap all at the same time, but rather a process that is based on your imagination to fulfill your ideas and the patience to wait for the right moment to act.

Your purpose is the essence of how you communicate yourself throughout your world, just as your feelings are the essence of your soul. The more you think about the thoughts that drive you, which must find their roots in your soul, the purpose for which you live your life becomes the outward expression of your most important ideas and dreams. It is essential to develop your thoughts and then discover your purpose to be fulfilled. The passion to which you commit to your purpose will find their truest ways of expression.

Will

Will is a deep seated desire to compel that which you want in the thought world to transpire into a physical reality. Will, though, remains an active ingredient that is only specific to the mind's eye, not existent in the reality of the physical experience. Therefore you need to use your will to maintain a steady thought, which will enable you to follow through with your intended purpose.

Your will is a quiet strength with infinite power. If, for instance, you have thought through your ambitions to get a job in a particular field and have settled on this aspect of your life as being that which you want most, it is your will that maintains the course to achieving it. Will is the strength that allows you to thwart away doubt and fear, and only look in the direction of reaching your goals.

We are a unique species, since as individuals and within collective society we have the ability to make up our minds and change them almost as quickly. But when you truly decide the course you want for yourself in this moment, the only way to ensure that you will achieve the end result (or at least carry on in the direction you wish to go) is through your ability to remain focused on that thing. If you know you are choosing the right direction for your life, your Will ensures that you will maintain the correct course.

Will is the subtle strength that allows that to happen. It is the power each of us has within us that is stronger than anything ever made in the physical world. It is a strength that has no need for rest or time to sleep. It starts out strong and remains steady through the time you access it. Will is the power that is immoveable and impenetrable; it is the essence of power, and you have within your mind the profound ability to tap this amazing resource

There is not a single distraction or overpowering thought that can penetrate the indomitable will of a person, not when one is committed to the very existence of the purpose for which it protects. When you shape your life, understand the seat of your soul, and then become part of the greater thinking force within the universe, it is up to your attention to will that allows you to see through your visions. Your will is virtually unshakable.

Unfortunately, though there is not another living entity that can cause you to break your will if you are steadfast in your resolve, the ability to break down your own walls of will is as easy as blowing an eyelash off your fingertip. Any sense of laziness or self-doubt not accompanied with the focus of your vision will ultimately erode the wall of will.

If you are one of the 50% of US citizens that is obese (according to the medical definition) then weight is likely a common issue for you. Or rather, getting back to your ideal weight is a goal to which you aspire. And this is a very significant example in the attempts to exercise your will. The moment you decide to lose the weight and get back to a healthier self-image, you have established the goal necessary to act on. But the plusher of exercise books, diet programs, and lose-weight-quick schemes is a testament to just how difficult the task of losing a few pounds is.

Losing weight is no more difficult than adding simple arithmetic. It is a process to which you commit. You must allow the intended goal to be reached without looking back at the origin of the goal. That is, when you decide it is time to lose weight and get back to your ideal health image, then you have to think through the idea, establish the purpose for the change, and simply allow your will to ensure that it is achieved.

It sounds so simple to just think about the loss of weight and then imagine that it will happen, but honestly, is there another way you will lose weight quicker and easier? You decide whether you set up a gym membership and plan a workout routine, you decide if you will eat the donut or the salad, it is your choice whether or not you drink the can of soda or glass of water. These are choices we make on a daily basis, and often are the central point to why we fail at losing a few pounds.

It is not your lack of will that causes you to stumble over your goal or prevents you from following through at all; it is your ability to convince yourself that you can let your guard down, cheat a little, or pick up on the diet at another, more convenient time. But this is the dangerous position you will always find yourself in if you continue to think of your will as a series of choices after you have made the original choice. Will is absolute, and it only knows what it has been directed to protect. But you are also quite easily capable of relieving your will of duty, just as a guard is relieved of his watch command.

Will is the power which allows you to think through your thoughts, establish a goal, and see to it that your goal is protected from any outside influence, even though the influence typically comes from within your own mind. It is not as if there is another person standing there and telling you to take a break, kick your legs up, eat the cake, and that it's okay, you can work out tomorrow. This almost never happens. It is our lack of accessing will that allows these other thoughts, the thoughts that focus on doing what is easy, and the thoughts that prevent us from facing a challenging endeavor, and instead allow us to opt out the moment we feel resistance or difficulty.

The process of a goal is the blueprint to achieving that goal but it is your will that allows the process to be completed.

Losing weight, getting an education, finding happiness, knowing truth – these are all easy ideas to reach in theory, yet we make it so difficult to attain any of our goals when we allow self-doubt and fear to infiltrate our vision and our goals. Anything you want to change about yourself, regardless of what it is, always falls into a process. It is a process to lose weight, just as it is a process to make your bed or do the dishes.

Once the idea or goal is established and you have a very good mental outline of that which you choose to commit to, it is then up to your strength of will that determines how easy, difficult, or impossible it will be to reach your goal. There are as many reasons to not do a thing as there are to do it, and it is your will that determines which reasons prevail. Even more, it is your will that prevents the disengaging ideas to even surface. If you want to be a better person spiritually, it is your will that will force that to fruition. If you want to be a better parent, it is the will to protect the idea and reach your ambition that allows this to come true.

Will is the power which forces the thing that you want to be created, using all of your internal qualities necessary to develop that thing into a physical reality. It is the power that ensures the carefully laid roots of thought and purpose are protected, and that the same roots are guaranteed to break through the surface into the representation of your physical world. When you have an idea, aspiration or goal, and think through the idea; it is your will that will guarantee the thing you think about is created.

Imagine deciding to lose weight. This is just one universal example that can be related to anything you want to change about you, and it is one of the most prevalent examples in modern society, yet it takes just as much mental capacity for establishing your goal and creating the imaging around the idea. The moment you decide to lose weight, you have made the decision to achieve your goal. If all things remained constant in the physical world as they do in the mental world, you would absolutely lose weight.

But there is another aspect to will that one must consider. It is the ability to adapt the changing physical landscape to protect the inner unwavering ideals. That is, when you think about the process you established to lose weight, you should make sure, above all else, that you continue to hold this process in your thoughts. You must never allow the process to be renegotiated until you have mastered the power of your will.

If you decide to lose weight, get a new job, or restart your education, you must, above all else, remain committed to seeing this through. For example, once you decide to lose weight, you would likely commit to an exercise routine; maybe walk a few miles every day and eat healthy meals. If you are like me, it is better to start small and work your way up to a more rigorous routine. The most important aspect of the routine is to make it become a habit.

Habit is what allows the will to remain steadfast without having to consciously focus on guarding the will to achieve results. When you first establish an exercise routine, you must be more focused on making sure you don't stray from the plan more than you are to the plan itself. But everyday that goes by where you are sticking to the plan of exercise, there is less of a need to rely on your will to ensure that the plan is followed through. Your sense of habit is allowing the pressure of guarding this change with your will, and it is almost as if you are establishing an autopilot for this goal. Quickly, it ceases to become a plan and begins to become your lifestyle.

Similarly, just as it is a process to establishing any goal or ambition, the other fact to this process is that change typically does not occur overnight. If losing weight is the goal, then it is quite impossible to reach your goal overnight. But statistically speaking, if you walk 3 miles every day, and eat healthier foods while making sure mathematically that you are taking in the maximum amount of daily calories or less based on your height and age, then it is only a matter of time before you will reach your ideal physical self-image. You must allow the process to be fulfilled in due time, rather than trying to seek immediate gratification; this is the only way to ensure real change in any aspect of your life.

If you focus on your life as a series of processes based on what you want for your life, it is quite possible to take away all guesswork or thoughts of chance altogether. You cannot graduate from college overnight, any more than you can become president just because you meet the age requirement, but if you are focused enough and use your mental strengths to understand what is right for you and what you want for your future, then you only need to activate your will to see your desires become a reality.

There are many inspirational stories that exemplify will, but none more simple and sincere than that of Dr. Glenn Cunningham, who at the age of 8 had almost perished in a fire. The same fire took the life of his 13-year-old brother. Glenn's entire lower body had been severely burned, to the point where doctors suggested amputating his legs, but Glenn, even at such a young age, refused to agree to the procedure. He insisted that he would walk again one day.

Every day for months, Glenn would drag his body across the grass to the fence in front of his house and then alongside it, trying to force his legs to work. Ultimately, he was able to do just that, and in a multiyear process, he was not only able to walk again, but he had become a two time Olympic athlete, winner of the national amateur athlete award, and is today still considered to be one of the best one-mile runners in history.

Dr. Cunningham did not have a special power or a magical wand to get his legs working again. He had the will to walk, the will to run, and the will to rise above preconceived limitations, even though the limitations seemed more likely and present than the reality of walking again. He practiced his will to achieve what his thoughts had produced, and he soon developed a process to reach this goal.

Surely, his process to success seemed ill conceived from the start, considering that doctors had all but guaranteed he would never walk again. If the doctors had been persuasive over Cunningham's own will, they would have taken his legs and his legacy.

But this is the power of what will can accomplish, even in the face of seeming defeat. There is a way to accomplish the purpose that you design for your life, assuming that you have a will that does not waver, a will that will not listen to the doubts of others, a will that will not succumb to the doubts of yourself, and a will that will not be denied the ability to force thought and purpose into reality.

Relationships

Relationships are the backbone of our individual existence. They serve as the method in which we learn, develop, and communicate our life to one another. Even the solitary man has relationships with those around him. If you are currently struggling with personal relationships, whether with a partner, family, friends or colleagues, it is likely you are dealing with issues that are completely internalized and have little to do with the other person in the situation. How you deal with your personal relationships is a reflection of how you understand your personal life. That is, if you are constantly surrounded by drama and chaos within relationships, it is likely that you are creating the drama you are witnessing.

You have the absolute power to attract a life partner or close relations with family and friends with all the qualities that you want and desire. How do you do this? First and foremost, you must know exactly the description and qualities you want in a partner or other relationships you develop. You should come up with a list of all the things that you would like to attract in people and write them down. You can write things such as loving, caring, encouraging, honest, and faithful. You can write anything that you can imagine. Only you know what you want. You can be as specific as to say that you want an attractive mate, you can list eye color, hair color, height, build, etc.

Once you have attracted the people that you desire, you will be surprised at all the traits that you have listed that your significant other has.

If you are currently in a relationship, please be aware that you cannot nor should you ask for a different partner to enter your life. This would be a contradicting element. This ill-intentioned desire would set off another Universal Law; The Universal Law of Karma. Always remember you get what you put out. And having a second individual enter into your life before you brought closure to another relationship may produce negative circumstances that could be harmful to everyone involved.

If you are in a relationship that you don't feel honors who you are, you must remove yourself from that relationship before you ask for your ideal partner. You should want to start off your new relationship in the best way possible, and begin free from negativity or doubt.

Now here is the part where action is taken. In order to attract the partner you desire, you must first believe that you are worthy of your partner. If you want to attract someone that is happy, then you must first become happy yourself. If you want to attract someone that is trustworthy, then you must be truthful yourself. If you want to attract a romantic partner, you must also appreciate romance within yourself. In order to attract your ideal partner with the qualities that you want, you must first become the person you want to attract.

The Law of Attraction will always bring together the perfect match based on the vibrations you extend from the base of your soul. This is an attraction-based Universe, and you get what you put out. Remember: like attracts like!

Next you must use your imagination. Imagine how you would feel if this person was in your life right now. How does it feel? Good feelings are the best way to attract all of the things that you desire most.

I would imagine myself on a beautiful island with the person that I desired. I would imagine walking hand and hand on the beach, just loving, talking, and enjoying each other. I would image what our life would be like at home, laughing, and enjoying each other's company, or just being happy when we see each other after a long day apart.

Use your imagination. Just sit and relax, and picture it in your mind like a movie; make it a vivid picture and make it as real as possible. It is best not to have a specific person in mind. Instead, let the Law of Attraction bring the person that you desire to you. Remember you do not have the ability to make someone want to be with you. Everyone has their own wants and desires, and you will only attract this ideal person into your life experience if they also want the same things as you.

You must then believe that this person will come into your life. You must see him or her with you now. You must say things like: I am happy to have the man or women of my dreams. I love him or her so much. I can't wait to get home to that person. This is the best way to get yourself into the thought process that he or she is here now. This will help you to send out a strong vibration to the universe that you already have what you desire and it will give you more of what you are feeling.

This is the point in the process where patience is most important. If you start to question (for example, why this person is not in your life yet?) no matter how long it has been since first dreaming of this relationship, you are giving attention to the lack of not having something, and the Universe will respond to your feelings of lack, giving you more of what you are giving your attention to. This is the point where resistance becomes a factor, and it will only take a longer period of time for you to receive what you are asking for.

You must BELIEVE! Believe in the fact that you will get exactly what you desire. Recall the past relationships you have had, and consider why they did not work out. It was always one reason or another, which supports the point that if the person you are with does not match the person you had envisioned to be with, then the result will always be friction within the relationship. A resistance will develop, and over time will ultimately lead to negative feelings and a break up.

Never concern yourself with how, when, or where you will meet
this person; the Universe will take care of those details for you. In fact,
think of the relationships that you have had in the past, and you will see
that you could never have recreated the moment you met. It was a
magic moment that came from nowhere, yet nonetheless changed your
life immediately. The Universe will choose the path in which you will
meet. You just need to stay focused on what you want in a partner and
know that you deserve to have whatever you want.

Personal Success

The true beauty of life is that everyone has the ability to be
personally successful. And the success you achieve is based on the
vision you have for yourself now and for your future. But defining that
success is an individual endeavor. No one is going to hand you the keys
to your own success. In fact, if you were magically teleported into your
own future with all the success you could imagine, you would be
further from true success than when you get there on your own merits.

The journey to self-discovery is a never ending one. There is no
singular destination to reach. Just as the universe is infinite it is size and
distance, so too is your path to your personal awareness. There is
always another point to go, another mountain to climb, another obstacle

waiting to be overcome. It is the challenges on the way to our goals that provide us with the knowledge and strength to move closer to our better selves; our true selves.

Your soul is the ultimate guide to finding strength and solitude and understanding the amazing Life force you are a part of. When you stop and understand the power within you and begin to feel your way through life rather than trying to think your way through, you will become a wiser person instantaneously. There are steps you must take in order to refine your self-image and continue to discover this power, but when you are committed to truly listening with your inner voice, you will be standing on firmer ground with a confidence that will never waver.

Your inner voice is the real guide with which you must begin your journey and nourish your soul with Truth, Love and Patience. You are growing the most valuable seeds ever produced that inevitably sprout up into your thoughts and provide the sense of clarity that will help develop the best within you to share externally. The seeds of your Soul are the equivalent of the California oaks growing mightily and tall, and will give rise to all that is great about you. There is no secret formula, no mysterious strike of luck or personal ambition that will guide you through the complexities of life.

You only need to tap into the greatest part of you; the part of you that connects every single person on the planet and is your lifeline to the Intelligent Universe. You are most certainly a special person and you must understand the importance in understanding your Soul, growing your strengths and allowing your inner voice to become the leading faction of your being. You cannot fail if you hold, Truth Love and Patience as your internal guide light. And when the moment seems difficult or negative emotions give rise within, the best thing to do is to recall what Truth, Love and Patience mean to you and the clouds of self-doubt, fear, and the unknown will give way to harmony.

And as you come to understand the power of your soul in relation to the life you live on earth, you begin to shape your thoughts that only harbor the best intentions, the most honest intentions. You begin to think clearer thoughts, find more meaningful purpose and develop a will that is immovable. You begin to shape a clearer mind that is fed the most powerful of life's intentions. When you truly start to develop pure thoughts stemming from the seat of your soul, you almost immediately begin to feel the powerful connection with everything in your world.

There is nothing as powerful as an individual who has made a commitment to themselves, who has dedicated their life to understanding themselves in their purest sense. To find the essence of you is a rewarding individual endeavor, but the impact you will have on the people around you will be as inspiring as the lessons you learn for yourself. You are the master of your fate, you define your destiny and only you alone can reach the highest points of your human evolution.

The life you want to live in this world will come true for you. It is virtually impossible for you to know what you want for your life and not find the ability to make that dream come true. It is as much a certainty as it is a mathematical equation. Life will guarantee that which you strive for as long as you strive to become a better part of Life itself.

I find myself constantly fascinated and internally moved with stories of inspiration. People just like you and me do some pretty amazing things, accomplish extremely difficult tasks and overcome seemingly impossible obstacles but the most inspiring aspect is that they are not super human. They do not have a special gift that others do not possess. They simply have a personal belief system that will not waver in the face of doubt, fear or seeming defeat. They know themselves better than most people and follow an inner guide that is connected to Life itself.

The ability of the individual to rise beyond their self-defined limitations is perhaps the most important element of any aspect of you. If Dr. Cunningham had considered for a moment on that hospital bed that the doctors might be right and that he would indeed never walk again, then his legs would have been removed and his life forever altered. But he found a strength that we all have yet few ever tap into. You must find your strength, know that it is always there for you to access and it will help you soar to unimaginable prosperity.

Society is the collection of unique individuals, from different walks of life converging together to establish an easier method of producing the physical necessities of life. Carl Jung spoke of this as the collective consciousness. The community itself begins to take on a sense of its own development, being less inclined to include the individual in its development. And the leading issue with many people living in the world's largest cities is that their individual freedom is being crushed by the hasty movement of the collective order and those that seek the power to make decisions. How could our belief in politicians become so distrustful that they have become the stereotypical "bad" guys when they are elected by the collective community and are supposed to be entrusted with the greater good of the community they lead? Because we have resigned ourselves to believe the false concept that external power reigns over the Soul.

And as Jung explains, the individual is in grave jeopardy of losing its very meaning if we continue on a course where the community matters more than the individual or man accepts externally what he internally knows is wrong: Where technological and sociological advances become more prominent than the individuals inner development. This is precisely why a mob mentality is a very sensitive and often dangerous entity. When one becomes part of a group that comprises many independent beings without proper order, the chaotic representation of the varying stages of development become strained and the course of direction unclear.

The rate of all undesirable behavior expressed by man is remarkably higher in the larger cities than they are in the smaller communities and this is precisely because there is an easier connection to see the individual's relationship within the community. In fact, in a small community, the individual is able to affect the direction of that community simply by having an invested part in the development of the community. But however you see your relationship in the world and where you want to go or what you want to become, you have to first realize that you are an amazing person and there is not another person on the planet that has something that you cannot develop internally. There are people that have a higher order of intelligence, a healthier physical strength, more money, but no one has more soul than any other. No one feels any different than you.

How you feel is the true guide and your place in the world is guaranteed, but you must believe in what you want to become. You must listen to your inner voice and allow it to guide you throughout the physical realm. You are not wrong and will never find struggle if you always aim to allow your soul to become more pure. Your soul is real and your relationship with the Intelligent Universe and success on earth is wholly dependent on allowing yourself to return to the purity of Life and in so doing, you will find magnificent beauty throughout your Life.